KNOCK ON WOOD

KNOCK ON WOOD

A COLLECTION OF SUPERSTITIONS ABOUT LOVE, LUCK, MONEY, HEALTH, AND MUCH MORE

LINDA SPENCER

Gramercy Books
New York

This 2000 edition is published by Gramercy Books™,
an imprint of Random House Value Publishing, Inc.,
201 East 50th Street, New York, New York 10022,
by arrangement with Rutledge Hill Press, Inc.

Gramercy Books™ and design are trademarks of
Random House Value Publishing, Inc.

Random House
New York • Toronto • London • Sydney • Auckland
http://www.randomhouse.com/

Printed and bound in the United States of America

A CIP catalog record for this book is available
from the Library of Congress.

ISBN 0-517-20621-8

8 7 6 5 4 3 2

It is the customary fate of new truths to begin as heresies and to end as superstitions.

—Thomas Henry Huxley

Table of Contents

PART THREE: *To Have or Have Not—Money*   55

PART FOUR: *Good Health Luck*   75

Introduction

Everyone is superstitious. It's human nature, even though most folks don't admit to being superstitious. Some folks don't even know they are superstitious. When you cover your mouth during a yawn you are practicing a superstition. When you place the salt shaker first on the dinner table you are enacting a superstition.

There's more to superstitions than a rabbit's foot. Do you know what precise kind of rabbit's foot to carry for good luck? Did you know that superstitions about garlic's healing powers, which are thousands of years old, are being scientifically proven effective?

Did you know that knocking on wood calls forth the tree gods to bring you good luck? Primitive people the world 'round knocked on wood—today, folks still do.

Superstitions have been handed down from one generation to the next by word of mouth ever since humans first stood on two legs. What's the secret of superstitions' lasting power? Superstitions touch our most primal needs. Superstitions are our first attempts to explain the cause and effect of events in everyday life—some of those events still defy modern science.

Superstitions also speak of a harmony—harmony with each other, harmony with the natural world. Today, we would do well to heed that message.

The superstitions gathered here are familiar and unfamiliar. They are organized around love, money, luck, health, birds, insects, flowers, trees, and animals—ancient beliefs about very real aspects of our modern-day lives. May you always have good luck.

Part One

Love Lost, Love Gained

L ove makes the world go 'round," goes the old saying. Perhaps, but we do know that love is as old as humankind. Long before folks figured out how to build a house or tame animals or plant crops, there was love. Love, attraction, the natural chemistry that occurs when a person meets the "right" partner happened and still happens—house or no house, crops planted or not, or in the case of today, jobs or no jobs.

Of course folks have always wanted everything to go "right" in their love lives—and they still do! The superstitions and beliefs collected here give you tips on how to have a happy love life.

Who is the right one for you? Does she love you? Does he love you? Why is it important for the best man to stand on the right side of the groom? Just how did leap year evolve? The answers and some useful tips for a happy love life are right here.

◆ Predictions

Have you tried a computer dating service, astrology, singles clubs, Club Med, and still haven't met the "right" mate for you? Take some tips from our ancestors. Be sure to follow these directions carefully.

MEN

ROLL UP A pair of your socks before you go to bed at night. It helps if the socks are *not* sweat socks you wore at the gym that morning. Name each sock after a lady you know. Put them under your pillow. Get into bed over the footboard, backward. Be careful not to injure yourself—that would be self-defeating. But if you just get into bed from the side, sticking your socks under your pillow won't tell you a thing. The lady you dream about that night (presumably one you named a sock after) is the one you will marry. Maybe one day she'll even wash your socks.

---◆---

FOR THOSE BACHELORS on a business trip, the next time you sleep in a strange bed *alone*, take the opportunity to find out whom you will marry. On the first night before you get into bed, name each corner of the bed with a woman's name. If you dream about one of the ladies named, you will marry her. This has a glitch. If you're worried about the big business meeting with the bankers the next morning, you might not sleep at all.

---◆---

THIS ONE TAKES some gymnastics. Take two apple seeds. Name each seed after a woman you know. Wet each apple seed, and put it on the upper lid of each eye. Wink as fast as you can. The apple seed that falls off your eyelid first is the name of the woman you will marry. Then, Adam-like, be sure to eat the apple.

WOMEN

THIS ONE MIGHT take a while to do, considering how few white horses there are around. Count the white horses you see. After you've seen ninety-nine, the next man you shake hands with will be the one you marry. A friend of mine tried this not with horses but cars. In fact, while she was driving through an intersection she saw her ninety-ninth white car and, her mind on other things, she hit the car in front of her. It was only a fender bender, but the owner (he was tall and handsome) and she exchanged telephone numbers. Six months later they eloped in a new Volvo, white of course.

◆

IF YOU HAPPEN to step on a man's toes, whether dancing or in a crowd, he is the man you will marry. This could lead to polygamy if you live in a city and use public transportation. But the next time you step on a man's toes, take a good look at him. He just might be Mr. Right.

◆

EVE DIDN'T HAVE any choice as to whom she gave the apple. Adam was the only guy around. But before you give your apple away, try this. Cut it in half and put all the seeds in a pan on the stove. Name each seed after a man you know. Heat the pan. The first seed to pop reveals the name of the man for you.

◆

IF THERE ARE many men in your life and you wonder which one you will marry, take twelve slips of paper and write on each slip the name of one of the men. Put the twelve slips into an envelope and sleep with it under your pillow. Each day draw a slip from the envelope at random. Rip it up and toss it away. The last slip of paper in the envelope has the name of the man you will marry. If you have more than twelve men in your life, what are you worried about?

◆ Omens

W

ill you marry within the year? Will you marry at all?
How can you find answers to these significant
questions? Today some folks consult an astrologer. But
here are some ways your forebears knew when or
whether they would marry.

◆

WOMEN

IF A WOMAN braids her hair and leaves out a strand, it is a sign she
will marry within the year. Don't make this happen. It must be
accidental. So put it in your head and forget about it. The next time
you're braiding your hair and you leave out a strand . . . well that
means good news.

◆

IF YOU ARE a young woman, make a pie. That's a tall order these
days. How many women, even middle-aged, make pies? But if you're
desperate to know when you'll marry, it's worth it. While trimming
the pie crust, if it falls *over* your hand, that is a sign you will marry
young.

◆

A WOMAN WHO puts on a bridal veil and holds orange blossoms
on any occasion, but not her own wedding, will never marry. Don't
try on your best friend's bridal veil, no matter how tempting.
Everyone knows you would look better in her veil and holding her
orange blossoms, but don't tempt fate!

◆

IF A WOMAN is fond of cats, she will be an old maid. If a woman likes cats better than dogs, that is another sign that she will never marry. Not to cast doubt on these two, but I know tons of married women who love cats. Why do most women love cats? Cats do their own laundry. In fact, they prefer to do their own laundry.

◆

A WOMAN WHO makes a good-looking bed will have a good-looking husband. And a woman who has an unkempt bed has someone's husband.

◆

IF YOU HAVEN'T met Mr. Right yet, but want to see his face, follow these steps. Find a well. Make sure it's not covered so that you can actually look down into it and see the water. On the night of a full moon, toss a penny into the well. The face you see at the bottom of the well is the man you will marry. It must be a full moon however. Moons greatly assist in matters of the heart.

◆

IF YOU HAVE a man in your life and you want him to remain interested in you and pop the big question, *never* let him carry your comb in his pocket. If you do, he's sure to lose interest in you. This goes back to the time when combs were made of iron. Ancient humans believed evil spirits lived in iron. Some say even in Italy today, a couple to wed will not go near iron together—such as scissors.

◆

MEN

IF A MAN dreams of the same woman three nights in a row, then she is the woman he is to marry. If a man dreams of the same woman three nights in a row, I want to know what perfume she was wearing when they first met!

THIS ONE IS awful, but it once was done. If a man puts sugar in his armpits and then sugar in his lady's drink, she won't resist him. Note, don't put the same sugar in your armpit and then in your lady's drink. She just might keel over.

THINK VERY SERIOUSLY before doing this one. There's no way around this superstition once you start the forces in motion. If you are a love-sick bachelor, the flower bachelor button can forecast your future in happiness, love, and marriage. Bachelor buttons have a magical influence over single men. Pick the flower early in the morning with the dew still on the petals. Put it in your pocket and do not look at it for twenty-four hours. If, after those twenty-four hours, the flower is still bright, fresh, still "true blue," you will have wedded bliss. If the flower has withered, your union will be long and sad. You cannot cheat here by putting the flower, wet with morning dew, in a plastic bag and putting the bag in your pocket. That would increase your chances of good news. The chances of a flower surviving twenty-four hours in a man's pocket and remaining fresh are very slim. Be careful with this one. In the old days most bachelors who enacted this superstition remained bachelors forever.

◆ Four-Leaf Clover

L egend has it that when Adam and Eve were booted out of the Garden of Eden, Eve did not leave empty-handed. She grabbed a four-leaf clover. Ever since, four-leaf clovers bring good luck, but if you follow these directions, a clover can help you find the right man.

There are a couple of ways to do this, but first, *find* a four-leaf clover. You can buy clover in the produce department of most supermarkets, but it's packed in square plastic containers—and that's a no-no. By the way, four-leaf clovers grow best in unkempt lawns. Also be sure the clover hasn't been sprayed with pesticides, our modern-day equivalent of evil spirits.

—◆—

THE EASIEST WAY to work this charm is to pin the newly-found clover over the door to your house. Don't use tape, that might break the charm. There's something about the clover's touching metal that makes the charm work. And besides, the ancients didn't have tape. The first unmarried man who walks through your door after you've hung the clover is the man you will marry.

—◆—

OR, YOU CAN eat the fresh clover. The first unmarried man you meet after eating the clover is your future husband.

—◆—

YOU CAN ALSO put the four-leaf clover in your shoe first thing in the morning. The first unmarried man you meet that day is your man. And besides, fresh clover is better than Odor-Eaters!

8

◆ A Kiss Is More Than a Kiss

The first couple to kiss on the lips found ecstasy—our lips are our most sensitive touch zone. Good news travels fast and by the time of Samson and Delilah, a kiss led to a man's getting a haircut. We don't know if Adam and Eve kissed (yet they must have made a connection somewhere), but we do know some folks like the Eskimos and Maoris never discovered the ecstasy and just stuck to rubbing noses.

◆

GOOD THINGS LAST and the "explanations" for why they are good abound. Some ancients even believed the air they exhaled was magical and contained part of their true soul. The good feeling from kissing on the lips came from mingling two souls. A *romantic* notion.

◆

WHAT ABOUT THE Romans? We know a good deal went on, or was taken off, at Roman orgies. But Roman kissing eventually swung from orgy to suspicion. Roman husbands kissed their wives at the end of the day. But not for good feeling—supposedly the kisses were to see if the wives had been drinking wine all day. Hardly romantic.

◆

WHETHER MINGLING SOULS or checking for wine breath, kisses have changed lives—even history. Besides Samson and Delilah, there's Anthony and Cleopatra, Mary Queen of Scots and the Earl of Bothwell, King Edward VIII and Mrs. Simpson, and even Donald Trump and Marla Maples.

9

◆ Lover's Knot/Bride's Bouquet

The wedding ceremony is over. Everything went as planned. The bride did not trip; the groom did not faint. Now they stand on the steps of the church. She is going to throw her bouquet of orange blossoms and streams of ribbons tied in little knots—lover's knots.

Supposedly a wish is held in each knot. This, by the way, is true of any knot anywhere. But a bride's bouquet is supposed to have many knots so she will have many good wishes for future happiness. And with the divorce rate so high these days, brides (and grooms) need all the good wishes they can get!

◆

WHEN THE BRIDE throws the bouquet, the common belief is the woman who catches it will be the next one to marry. But purists say something different. The next time you're at a wedding and you catch the bouquet follow these steps: Right after you catch the bouquet, make a silent wish. Take the bouquet home and untie one of the knots. As you untie one of the knots, your wish will come true— maybe a new age sensitive man will materialize before your eyes!

◆

KNOTS AND WEDDINGS generally go together. In India, before the ceremony every knot on the garments of the bride and groom is unfastened. This is to let out the evil spirits who were going to spoil the couple's wedding day. The actual tying of the lover's knot takes place in the marriage ceremony. The untying of all knots on the bride's and groom's garments could be a problem in Western marriages. If you are going to have an Indian-style marriage, I suggest the bride wear a sari and the groom a Nehru suit.

IN EARLY ENGLAND, just before the wedding celebration, every knot on the clothes the bride and bridegroom were wearing was loosened—but not untied. Those Brits were cautious even then.

THE KNOT'S A symbol of love, honor, friendship, and indissoluble union—all those good qualities do make a great deal of sense. In ancient times the knot was the only way to fasten anything—there were no such things as buttons, zippers, or Velcro. In primitive times, people who could tie knots were considered "magic" people because the knot—something today almost every three-year-old child learns to do—was magical.

ONE LAST THOUGHT about knots: The next time you're feeling sorry for yourself for whatever reason, remember the emperor of China in the movie *The Last Emperor*. He was never taught how to knot his own shoes—he learned how to tie a knot only after being deposed. Imagine having been ruler of China, lived in opulence, lost all, and you can't even do a simple thing for yourself as tie your own shoes. Be thankful you can tie a knot—whether it be a lover's knot or not.

◆ How to Insure Happiness When You Marry

Kisses lead to weddings and weddings have a slew of superstitions. For instance, to insure a happy marriage you must have at least ten witnesses to the event. Unseen jealous evil spirits lurk about at weddings to destroy the couple's happiness. (Given the high divorce rate these days, evil spirits must be working overtime.) Ten witnesses outwit the jealous demons by confusing them as to who's getting married. The ancient Romans even enacted a law requiring ten witnesses for the marriage to be legal. So even if you decide to elope, be safe, round up a gang of at least ten.

◆

OF COURSE THE groom is never supposed to see the wedding dress until he sees his bride in it at the wedding. This evolved from a time when the groom never even laid eyes on his bride until *after* the ceremony when her veil was lifted.

◆

THE WEDDING DRESS in the Western world is usually white, the sign of joy; black is usually the sign of sadness. It's reversed in the Orient. To be sure she will be happy in her marriage, the Western bride *must* carry orange blossoms—the ultimate fertility symbol. Orange trees are evergreen, and they blossom and fruit simultaneously. Even today brides go to great lengths to carry orange blossoms. A friend was married in January in Alaska—not exactly a time or place for orange trees to flourish. She had her bouquet flown in from Seattle. The hitch was the groom was allergic to orange blossoms, which he had never seen until that day, and sneezed through the entire ceremony.

◆

SOME ANCIENT BELIEFS are best left in the past, such as the bride covering her face with a veil. Magically, under the veil she was supposed to shed her old self and take on her new identity as a wife, all of this during the ceremony. The veil also expresses humility toward the groom, which the ancients believed made for a good wife. Women's lib, where were you?

◆

CUSTOM DECREES THE bride always stand to the left of the groom during the ceremony, leaving the groom's right hand free—just in case he has to draw his sword quickly to defend himself and his bride from jealous rivals. Sword wearing is not popular today, I'm happy to report. Besides, jealous rivals now do more sinister things—like cancel the couple's reservations at the planned honeymoon retreat.

The best man stands on the groom's right, just behind him. The best man should be the groom's best friend, pal through thick and thin. In the old days the best man even helped his friend capture the bride. At the ceremony he stood nearby to protect the couple and see that they sped off safely on their honeymoon. He was dressed similarly to the groom—a custom that is still followed. This helped confuse those unseen evil spirits.

—◆—

BRIDESMAIDS ATTEND THE bride dressed in similar dresses, but never white. But again, this was to confuse the evil spirits. It can be an awesome task to get five bridesmaids to agree on one dress style and color. "Always a bridesmaid but never a bride" is a common belief. But the superstition can be broken—if you are only a bridesmaid seven times (keeping in harmony with seven monthly moon cycles), the next wedding will be yours. However, by that time you might be fifty years old. But better late than never.

—◆—

ACCORDING TO TRADITIONS worldwide, the ceremony was and is even today performed under a canopy or "cere-cloth." This was held over the couple to prevent evil spirits from raining on them. Today we have evil spirits in the form of acid rain and ultra-violet rays to worry about.

◆ Third Finger Left Hand

Before the sign of the cross scared off vampires, the unbroken circle of a ring protected us from evil spirits. What evil spirits? Disharmony and unhappiness. And it's still bad luck for a married couple to remove their wedding rings. There's some truth to this. During a fight, a couple I know threw their wedding rings into the garden. Lawyers were consulted; divorce seemed imminent. A friend found the rings with a metal detector. With the return of the rings the couple made up. Nine months later a set of twins was born. Harmony certainly had been restored!

◆

WEDDING RINGS ARE worn in most cultures on the third finger left hand because that's the "heart finger." It started with the ancient Egyptians. Supposedly a vein ran from the heart to the top of the third finger on the left hand. Anything evil that touched that finger would be felt by the heart. Whether that meant the touch produced heart palpitations, a heart murmur, or heart burn is anybody's guess. But the belief was so strong that Greek and Roman physicians stirred medicines with the heart finger. If the potions were poisonous their hearts would tell them. Let's hope they washed their hands. Later, Christians believed the thumb and first two fingers of the left hand symbolized the Trinity, so the heart finger nearest the Trinity was just the place for a wedding ring.

◆

ANGLO-SAXON MEN STATED their intentions up front and that apparently led to the engagement ring. They put a ring on their betrothed's right third finger while courting and during the wedding moved it to the heart finger. Donald Trump was simply following tradition when he gave Marla Maples that rock-sized diamond.

15

◆ Wedding Cake and Fertility

Wedding cakes, originally dry, tasteless biscuits made of flour, salt, and water, were believed to give the newly married couple plenty of children and happiness. Once the bride and groom shared a piece of biscuit, the remainder was broken over the bride's head. Let's assume the biscuit was always freshly baked. Guests scrambled for crumbs in the hope that they, too, would share in the blessings. This could be a bit messy today, since wedding cakes tend to be moist and gooey.

◆

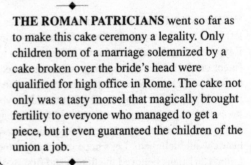

THE ROMAN PATRICIANS went so far as to make this cake ceremony a legality. Only children born of a marriage solemnized by a cake broken over the bride's head were qualified for high office in Rome. The cake not only was a tasty morsel that magically brought fertility to everyone who managed to get a piece, but it even guaranteed the children of the union a job.

◆

THINGS WERE A bit more staid and tidy at Anglo-Saxon wedding feasts. A huge basket of small dry biscuits was passed around. Each guest took one and the rest went to the poor. It took a Frenchman who attended such a feast to change things and invent the wedding cake as we know it today. He piled up the biscuits into one mound and poured icing over top.

SINGLE WOMEN STILL take home a piece of the wedding cake and put it under their pillows, believing they will wed the men in their dreams. With the influence of the new age, this custom has undergone some alterations. I know a single woman who put the cake in the freezer for seven months (keeping in harmony with the seven moon cycles), and then zapped it in the microwave on defrost before putting it under her pillow. Believe it or not she married a radiologist.

◆ Rice, Grain, Sweet Nuts, and Fertility

A story told here in Maine is that back in the thirties when times were tough, a couple both were from large families, had a very modest, but proper wedding. After the ceremony they stood on the steps of the church while the family snapped pictures with their Brownie cameras. The best man had distributed a small handful of store-bought rice to each guest to shower the couple. But what hadn't been foreseen was the ten-pound sack of beans the kids on the roof had. Since rice was not grown here, the kids did the best they could and dumped the beans on the couple as they left the church. Those kids probably had no idea why adults shower a married couple with farm produce in the first place. They had the right idea, but the wrong stuff. A sack of beans just doesn't have the magical powers rice or grain does to expel evil and bestow happiness and fertility. The ancients believed the fertility of the grain and rice was magically transferred to the couple on whom it falls.

The couple showered with beans did have one child, after being married seven years. That child had two kids, and each of them had two kids. So today the couple has two grandchildren and four great-grandchildren. But around here some say that's not many offspring at all considering both were from large families. It was "them beans," they comment darkly.

◆

TODAY PEOPLE STILL throw rice, sometimes confetti, but rarely wheat or barley. The Romans started the confetti throwing, which in their day was actually sweet meats—nuts and sugared almonds. The paper confetti of today is considerably neater than sticky almonds.

18

◆ Throwing Old Shoes

Why are old shoes tied onto the back of a car today along with tin cans or anything else that rattles? To drive away evil spirits, of course, and to scare away those supposedly well-meaning "friends" who want to follow you and your beloved on your honeymoon.

———◆———

BEFORE CANNED GOODS and automobiles, people threw old shoes at the newly married couple. That could be dangerous today, considering the weight of a Reebok; it's not the same as throwing a sandal. At one time people threw old shoes after anybody starting on a trip. Ben Jonson addressed this in his lines, "Hurl after me an old shoe/I'll be merry whatever I do."

———◆———

SHOES WERE SUPPOSED to ensure good luck and plenty of children because people believed the soul of the person who wore the shoes lived in them. Mingling souls was always supposed to be good luck, even through shoes. Where the soul of a person lived before people wore shoes, no one has yet been able to fathom.

———◆———

SHOES WERE ALSO a symbol of possession, and the bride's family's throwing their shoes at the couple indicated they gave up possession of her. Remember ladies, at one time women were chattel. Similarily, newly married women presented a pair of their shoes to their husbands to reaffirm their subservience. Groan! At least things have changed; these days women don't give their shoes to their spouses, even if they have 600 pairs.

◆ Mysterious Spaces—Thresholds

The threshold—that middle space that's neither inside or outside the door—is supposed to be inhabited by thousands of spirits. Some think the spirits are evil, some think they are good.

—◆—

TODAY IT'S TRADITION for the groom to carry the bride over the threshold—the ancient Romans actually started the practice. The threshold was sacred to the Roman goddess Vesta. She was the goddess of virginity. The Romans thought it was not proper for a virgin about to lose her maidenhood to touch the threshold. But today all brides get carried over the threshold—virgins or not. Now that's progress!

—◆—

IN EARLY ENGLAND even the chapel threshold was an object of superstition. Bad luck came to the newlyweds who stepped over the chapel threshold separately. If they did not cross in tandem, the one who went first would die first—and soon.

—◆—

SOME FOLKS BELIEVE to this day that if the groom doesn't cross the chapel threshold first, his bride will boss him their entire married life. Brides, step quickly!

—◆—

SO BELIEFS ABOUT thresholds can go either way. Some say it's good luck to step right on the threshold (the ground part of the threshold—the entire space is considered the threshold) when leaving the house. Others say it's bad luck—that demons live there.

IF YOU'RE UNDECIDED on how to handle thresholds in your life, consider the biblical stories in the books of Judges, 1 Samuel, and 1 Kings. Terrible things happen to people at thresholds in those books; people get cut up, a baby dies. This space is not to be played with. Newlyweds take heed and step lightly!

◆ Honey & Moons

After the knot is tied, off you go on a honeymoon. If you plan it right, no one will bother you, much less be able to find you. That is the ideal honeymoon and an ancient tradition.

◆

THE HONEYMOON ACTUALLY comes from a time when immediately following the ceremony the newlyweds drank mead (wine and honey) for a moon cycle—thus "honeymoon." The mead was supposed to make them fertile—progeny being the goal of marriages in primitive and ancient times. Love came later.

◆

CONSEQUENTLY, DURING THIS "honey" of a time, if the couple should argue, that's bad luck for the marriage. Probably not many arguments took place in primitive times since women were taught to "obey" their husbands. Thank goodness that custom is waning.

COUPLES DIDN'T STAY home to drink mead for a moon cycle, because in those days a man often stole his bride-to-be from her family. I repeat, ladies, we were once considered chattel. The groom would carry off his bride to some distant hiding place. The moon cycle time, which incidentally we now call a month, was long enough that her family would, from sheer exhaustion, cease their search. While her family searched, she and he drank mead and did what married couples still do today.

◆

THESE DAYS, WITH global travel what it is, it's hard for newlyweds to hide. A Maine couple told no one of their honeymoon plans, despite pleas from friends for the information. They married in June and took off down the road. They ended up in Tahiti and, while in a restaurant sipping Polynesian cocktails (not mead), ran into a couple from their Maine neighborhood! The world really is shrinking. To guarantee a "hidden" honeymoon these days try space travel.

◆ Leapin' Women's Lib

The belief that women may propose marriage every four years really didn't take hold until the thirteenth century. Supposedly Queen Margaret of Scotland decreed that every four years a woman could propose to any man she wanted. He could refuse only if he were engaged. If he defied the law, he was liable for a 100-pound fine. This leap-year decree was a leap ahead for women's rights, but it didn't last long.

—◆—

MAGISTRATES, WHO WERE all men of course, soon altered the decree. A woman could exercise the privilege of leap year only by indicating her intentions—by wearing a scarlet petticoat clearly visible at the hem. This gave the man a chance to run the other way.

—◆—

ANOTHER VERSION IS that St. Brigid and the nuns in her Irish convent (it was a time when nuns could marry) nabbed St. Patrick one day to complain how unjust it was that a woman never had the right to choose her mate. St. Patrick suggested women have the right to choose for a full year every seven years. Brigid protested, they settled on four years. Brigid proposed to St. Patrick. Having taken the vow of celibacy, he refused, but gave her a silk dress. For generations rejected Irish women were given a silk dress as a sop for their feelings. No comment.

Part Two

Good Luck and Bad

Sometimes everything in life goes your way. Everything clicks—your love life, your work, your finances, your health. The ancients would say it's because you have a horseshoe hanging in your house. Or you are carrying a lucky rabbit's foot or you're careful never to break a mirror.

Good luck is what everyone wants. No one wants trouble in life and most of us believe if we just do things right, we will have good luck. If we wish on that shooting star at the "right" time—our wish will come true.

But do you know the right kind of rabbit's foot to carry? Do you know how to protect yourself and your family from the evil eye? Do you know how to undo the seven years' bad luck that happens when you break a mirror? When *is* the right time to "wish upon a star"?

Here are all the answers to such questions and helpful tips to prevent bad luck. Many of these superstitions are as old as the hills. Some are adapted to invention—such as the umbrella.

May you and yours have good luck always.

◆ The Rabbit's Foot—Good Luck or Bad?

I t's a common complaint: "I carry a rabbit's foot, but it hasn't brought me any good luck." What to do? Carry your rabbit's foot only in your right pocket? The important consideration here is: Are you carrying the *right* rabbit's foot?

◆

A RABBIT'S FOOT is the most popular and most commonly used good luck charm. Millions of people spend millions of dollars yearly buying a rabbit's foot—usually at a drugstore or convenience store. But they buy the *wrong* foot. And when bad luck comes the poor rabbit gets blamed. Most people don't know that carrying around the small front paw of a rabbit won't bring you good luck. Only—and make sure you get this clearly—only carry around *the left hind foot of a rabbit killed at the full of the moon by a cross-eyed person*. Such a rabbit's foot is an infallible talisman. Such a rabbit's foot is also very hard to come by. How many cross-eyed persons do you know who will take time from their busy schedules to go cut off the left hind foot of a rabbit during a full moon?

◆

ALL SORTS OF people carry a rabbit's foot—whether the correct rabbit's foot or not. A well-known crusader for nuclear disarmament and environmental issues carries a rabbit's foot as she flies around the world on speaking engagements. Most actors and actresses keep a rabbit's foot in their make-up kits and stroke it for good luck before going on stage.

◆

THE RABBIT'S COUSIN, the hare, on the other hand, is associated with bad luck. From ancient times rabbits and hares have been confused, and even today most people don't know the difference between a rabbit and a hare.

For a quick guide, remember the rabbit is smaller than a hare, has shorter ears and legs, and lives in a burrow. Bambi's best friend Thumper was a rabbit. So was Peter, the fellow who defied his mother and went into Mr. McGregor's garden. Hares are larger than rabbits and they have long ears with black tips and powerful hind legs. They live homeless in the open and depend on speed for safety. Hares never made it into the old children's stories.

MAYBE IT'S BECAUSE baby hares are born with hair and with their eyes wide open (kind of weird, feisty looking creatures), or maybe because hares are nocturnal creatures that gather together and sit in the moonlight, but for some reason the ancients believed that hares were evil. Hares supposedly consort with witches. Hares and the full moon have the power to change sex. (Quite a power!)

IF A HARE crosses your path, you will have a disappointment. If a hare runs by your house, there will be a fire. The list goes on. Today many still believe that if a hare crosses in front of a pregnant woman, the child she is bearing will be born with a harelip—unless the woman quickly tears a slit in one of the undergarments she is wearing.

BUT THE GOODY-GOODY rabbit cousin means good luck and prosperity—especially the white rabbit. Alice knew what she was doing when she followed that white rabbit. In fact, white rabbits were often given to children in the hopes that the children would grow into prolific and prosperous adults.

—◆—

SOMEHOW THE WHITE rabbit got attached to Easter and the Easter bunny was born along with, several centuries later, Cadbury chocolate Easter eggs. Perhaps the legend in northern countries that the white rabbit emerged with the Easter moon spawned the belief. In Germany the white rabbit was made an Easter goddess who laid eggs for good children on Easter Eve. Today we have a white Easter bunny that leaves eggs for good children—chocolate eggs, jelly beans, and other assorted confections. Rabbit eggs anyone? Chickens move over!

◆ Lucky Metal—Horseshoes

Finding a horseshoe means good luck. Nothing evil lurks in or around a horseshoe. For good fortune always and forever, all you have to do is find a horseshoe with the open hoof space toward you. Then all your troubles are over—you are going to get that big job, your mother-in-law will move out, your kids will behave, and if you're unmarried Mr. or Ms. Right will come along. Horseshoes are better than winning the lottery. If you win the lottery you have the problem of how to spend the money and figuring the taxes you owe. If you find a horseshoe with the hoof space open toward you, even that problem is solved.

◆

THE TROUBLE THESE days is that there are more cars than horses, and the chances of finding such a horseshoe (any horseshoe for that matter) are as slim as winning the lottery. And unfortunately no superstition exists about cars—such as if you find a tire, a left rear tire while walking on the west side of a dirt road, then all your problems are over. The modern age has certain deficiencies.

◆

BUT DESPITE THE demise of the horse as a means of travel, beliefs about horseshoes are still widespread. If you dream of a horseshoe, you will receive unexpected money. Maybe then you *will* win the lottery.

◆

IF YOU HANG a horseshoe in your bedroom, you will be protected against nightmares. Be careful not to tack it up where it might fall on your head. If that happens you won't have to worry about nightmares, you'll be dead.

THE GREEKS MADE the first horseshoes to protect the feet of their horses, animals they considered sacred. But the U-symbol, half-circle, or crescent was around long before Greek civilization came to the fore. The stones at Stonehenge, thanks to the Druids, are arranged in a horseshoe shape. The shape is connected to the ancients' perception of the sun's movements.

THE HORSESHOE SYMBOL, with points up, represents masculine powers, with points down, feminine powers. The symbol always has been considered potent and protective.

THE GREEKS AND Romans tacked horseshoes on walls to protect themselves from the plague. The last letter in the Greek alphabet, Omega, is a horseshoe shape. Most country folks here in Maine have a horseshoe tacked over the front door and one nailed to a beam in the barn for good measure. And the horse that wins the Kentucky Derby gets a U-shaped wreath of roses hung over its neck. If I had a choice between a horseshoe with its ancient history of good luck or five free lottery tickets, I'd take the horseshoe. The odds are better!

◆ The Evil Eye

"If looks could kill, his would have killed the treasurer," my friend Sarah said, reporting a recent business meeting she had attended.

Unknowingly Sarah, a young executive, was referring to a universal belief that dates back to our most primitive days—the evil eye. Another variation of this belief is the expression: "She gave him a dirty look."

◆

FORTUNATELY THE BELIEF in the evil eye evolved without sexism—today both men and women can give the "eye" to someone. That was not always the case. The ancients believed only women had the evil eye. In fact, in Roman days a cult of professional witches advertised they each had the evil eye and hired out to bewitch folks' enemies. Hey—a woman has to earn a living and witchery is one of women's oldest professions!

◆

IN MEDIEVAL TIMES people were so frightened of the evil eye that anyone with a peculiar look in his or her eyes was liable to be burned at the stake. It was during medieval times that cross-stitch embroidery was popular as an amulet. If you hung a sample of cross-stitch embroidery in your house, anyone with the evil eye could not enter. It's a variation on the belief that the symbol of the cross scared away vampires. Usually the embroidery was hung inside over the entrance to the house. Nowadays an embroidery sampler is considered a decoration.

◆

SALIVA IS THE universal amulet to protect against the evil eye. It's easy enough—if you feel the evil eye on you, simply spit. Be careful where you spit, however, your boss might not understand if you spit during a meeting with the bankers! Somehow spitting magically prevents harm. Why liquids have traditionally held so much power no one knows, but the belief that a baby is protected from the evil eye by its mother's squirting breast milk into the baby's eyes is still held by many today in rural Europe.

———◆———

THE IDEA OF the evil eye goes back to the belief in dragons. Dragons supposedly had emerald eyes that could paralyze victims simply by staring at them. King Arthur, where are you? How the evil eye was associated with humans we simply don't know. Somehow the belief also got transferred to reptiles in general. In India, for instance, the cobra, which is considered both sacred and evil, is believed to have the power to immobilize victims simply by staring at them.

———◆———

OF COURSE THE poor peacock has suffered down through the ages, simply because it has so many "eyes" on its tail. In the 16th century liars and cheats were bedecked with garlands of peacock feathers. And even today theater people believe peacock feathers to be bad luck—all those evil eyes!

———◆———

RINGS THROUGH THE earlobes were also supposed to protect people from the evil eye. Sailors, however, evolved another belief about rings through the earlobes—before sonar when a sailor's eyesight often determined if he got a job, many sailors pierced their earlobes and wore one or two earrings to give them good eyesight.

———◆———

DOWN THROUGH THE ages, other eye superstitions developed. If your right eye itches, you will receive a letter. If your left eye twitches you will have bad luck.

PEOPLE WERE AND still are judged by their eyes. If you meet a person with eyes too close together—watch out. This person is bound to be selfish and dishonest. Likewise watch out for people with "beady" eyes—small eyes that resemble little glass beads. Those people are greedy.

◆

PEOPLE ARE SINCERE if they can "look you straight in the eye," but lying to you if their eyes wander while talking with you. But beware—lie detector tests show no basis for this belief. A person can look another in the eye and, according to the polygraph, still be lying. There's just no telling anything about a person these days!

◆ Mirror, Mirror on the Wall— Don't Break

Why does a broken mirror bring bad luck? It's connected to that Greek fellow Narcissus. One day, according to the myth, he saw his own image in a stream, fell in love with himself, languished, and died. The idea of vanity had evolved! False vanity or not, the ancients believed any object that reflected a human's image was "divine." These folks would be impossible in a Hall of Mirrors at an amusement park today.

◆

IRONICALLY, WHEN THE mirror was invented (1300s AD) the beliefs grew—even though the mirrors were man-made, they still held magical power! Unfortunately that power was evil. Snow White's step-mother and her famous mirror are an example.

◆

TODAY, THE BELIEFS about mirrors are still strong. Break a mirror, and you will have seven years of bad luck. (The seven years is a hold-over from the ancients' observing the seven phases of the moon.)

◆

IF YOU DO break a mirror, take heart. There is a way to reverse the bad luck. Gather up the broken pieces and toss them in a stream. But be careful not to fall in love with your image in the stream! If you don't live by a stream, pound the broken pieces so fine no mortal can ever again see in the mirror. My friend Ted broke a mirror on New Year's Day—not a good omen. He took no chances. He carefully pounded the mirror pieces into a powder. Then he scattered the powder over the stream. As the granules settled on the water, he chanted three times, "good luck." His fastidiousness has paid off. He hasn't had any bad luck this year.

———◆———

SUPERSTITIONS ABOUT UNBROKEN mirrors also still exist. Some folks cover mirrors after a death in the family. They fear the soul that departed will enter the mirror and the soul won't make it to heaven.

———◆———

IT'S RECOMMENDED TO always hang a cloth over a bedroom mirror when going to bed. If you don't, your soul could be caught in the mirror while you sleep—it's always best to keep your soul in bed with you.

———◆———

EVERYONE SHOULD BEWARE of a person whose image does not reflect in a mirror. That person is a vampire, especially if he (or she) is from an old royal family in Translvania!

◆ Knock on Wood

T hese days everyone knocks on wood. Maybe it has to do with the economy. Recently while I was in the bank, I watched in amazement as one of the vice presidents, while talking to a customer, proceeded to knock on wood! Let's hope they were not talking about the economy.

———◆———

THE BANKER WAS following a custom as universal and as old as the hills. Knocking on wood, or touching wood as some Europeans refer to it, is done to prevent bad luck. It also is done after boasting—humbleness still being a virtue, despite the 1980s.

———◆———

ALL THIS KNOCKING on wood started with trees and how the ancients regarded trees (from whence wood comes). Some trees change with the season—some trees are evergreen. The ancients believed gods and goddesses lived in trees. Some of these deities brought on seasonal changes and could protect you from misfortune. Those deities who lived in evergreen trees even gave everlasting life. Tree gods and goddesses were powerful, and how you fared in life depended on how you approached them. Good communication was important even then. Touching the trees was the universal approach.

Trees, and later wood, have been considered sacred from the time humans first stood upright. Christians have the Cross, Buddhists the Bodhi-Tree, and the Hebrews the Tree of Knowledge.

———◆———

IT'S TOO BAD that today we lack the ancients' respect for trees. We might have more wilderness left.

◆ Ladders in Life

id you ever wonder why you'll have bad luck if you walk under a ladder? It bothers the spirits who live in that triangle formed when a ladder is leaning against a building. That triangle is sacred—so beware.

———◆———

COUNTERCHARMS DO EXIST that can prevent that bad luck: Cross your fingers when walking under a ladder. Some folks claim you have to cross all of your fingers on both hands. They take no chances. Others say cross only the fingers of your left hand. Whatever, it's best to cross at least two fingers when you walk under a ladder.

◆

ANOTHER COUNTERCHARM IS to close the fist of your left hand and place your thumb between your index and middle finger. This symbol wards off bad luck. But be careful doing this gesture, it could easily be misconstrued.

◆

LADDERS HAVE APPEARED in people's dreams for centuries. If you dream you are climbing up a ladder, you will succeed in life. If you dream you are descending a ladder, you will fail in life. But don't despair—there's a remedy. If you dream you are descending a ladder, and then dream of climbing a ladder, your good luck is restored. Soon you will overcome your failures.

◆

LADDERS ARE ONE of those universal symbols—stories about ladders exist among all peoples. The ancient Egyptians put ladders in tombs for the dead. The Hebrews record Jacob's dream about a ladder in Genesis. Jacob didn't climb the ladder, rather the "angels of God were ascending and descending on it." But that dream still brought great luck—Jacob's family grew to be a nation!

◆ Umbrellas & Good Luck

My friend Tom, a lawyer for a popular rock singer, always carries an umbrella—snow or sunshine, rain or sleet. He sometimes dyes his hair green, occasionally wears jeans ripped at the knees, but he carries an umbrella. He claims umbrellas bring good luck—even the Mini-Totes. I attributed Tom's superstition to his growing up in Seattle where it rains most of the time.

◆

BUT I NOW know folks have always believed an umbrella, or canopy in ancient days, brought good luck. Such an "overhead" protection kept away the evil spirits. Tom's been a traditionalist all these years!

◆

MINI-TOTES WEREN'T AROUND in ancient Babylon in the eleventh century BC—neither were lawyers for rock singers. But, kings, queens, priests, and priestesses walked under a small canopy—a woven cloth supported by four poles. A servant carried each pole and the canopy lay suspended just above the heads of personages when they mingled with the masses. Each corner of the canopy represented the four corners of the Earth. Apparently the evil spirits never thought of getting under the canopy by going around the sides!

◆

TODAY THE WORLD puts a plastic bubble over important persons when they go out among the masses. It's gruesome to think about, but nowadays we have evil spirits in the form of would be assassins.

◆

IT WASN'T UNTIL the eighteenth century that anything like the umbrellas we have today were invented and used by the common man—ladies did not carry umbrellas. But the beliefs stuck. The first "modern" umbrellas were made with eight ribs—symbolic of the four points of the compass, doubled for good luck.

The day came, of course, when a brave woman carried an umbrella, which spawned the parasol. Soon a language evolved— the language of the umbrella. This "language" enabled a woman and man to flirt behind a chaperone's back! Today such subtle customs aren't practiced. A woman doesn't need an umbrella to flirt!

——◆——

BUT IT'S STILL bad luck to open an umbrella inside—Mini-Tote or not. Umbrellas are and always have been shields for use in the open air. The umbrella spirit is insulted if you open it up while you're inside. Also remember that umbrellas used to have a stiff spring and swoop open. Such an umbrella was bound to poke someone or knock over a fragile vase—creating bad luck in the way of bad feelings. But with the Mini-Tote, the chances of knocking over an heirloom vase are slim. But still . . . I recommend waiting until you get outside. Tom, the very successful lawyer, does!

41

◆ Lucky Breaks

That's a lucky break," is what folks around here were saying when a resident won the tri-state lottery. Believe it or not, this expression harkens all the way back to the days when we all lived in caves!

◆

EVIL SPIRITS LURKED everywhere and were always trying to interfere in everybody's lives. But it didn't take much to fend off the spirits. One ritual, guaranteed to scare off the evil, was to take a stick and snap it in the middle to make a loud noise. The noise scared away evil-doers. This was usually done before a hunt. If the hunt went well, everyone knew the breaking of the stick was a "lucky break." If the hunt was a failure, the breaking of the stick was a "bad break." Hindsight proved profound even then.

◆

THERE'S A MODERN day enactment of this belief—without using sticks. Stray sticks are not easy to find in our urban-oriented world. Folks snap their fingers or knuckles to make a crackling noise. Evil spirits or not, I've seen men do this before shipping out to war. I've seen high school athletes crack their knuckles before the big game. I've seen executives (both men and women) crack their knuckles in business meetings. It seems we humans always want a lucky break. Some beliefs die hard!

◆ Sweeping Luck—Brooms

The beliefs that have survived in the world of superstitions are not always kind to women. The belief about witches is an example. We realize today that witches in the time of our primitive ancestors were probably women who had herbal knowledge and were familiar with solar and lunar cycles—knowledge history has not always attributed to women. But the erroneous common belief today is that witches do evil and ride brooms. They don't drive Toyotas or Yuppie vans; they ride brooms—and not just on Halloween. How witches and brooms got connected no one knows—except that the broom is associated with magical spells. Unfortunately, those spells are mostly bad luck spells. But if you follow these tips, you can insure yourself against the evil spirits lurking in and around brooms.

◆

NEVER, NEVER TAKE a broom along when you move. Throw out your old broom and buy one for your new home. In fact it's good to always take a loaf of bread and a new broom into your new home. This will assure you good luck and happiness.

◆

IT'S BAD LUCK to lean a broom, new or old, against a bed. The evil spirits in the broom will somehow cast an evil spell on the bed. No one wants bad luck in bed.

◆

IF YOU DROP a broom, you will soon have company. It's best just to pick up the broom and sweep up a bit just in case company drops in.

IF YOU DROP a broom and you are single, don't step over the broom. Stepping over the broom insures you will never marry. This is true for women and men. Also don't step over a broom if you are pregnant. Your baby will be hairy. Brooms have a wide range of powers.

SINCE BROOMS HAVE such magical powers, naturally people have superstitions about sweeping. There is a time to sweep and a time not to sweep. Don't sweep the house at night. This insults the spirits of the dead and they will work bad luck on you. Only sweep during daylight hours. This is an excellent reason not to clean house after a long day at the office.

THERE IS A way to sweep: Don't sweep dust out the front door. You are sweeping all your good fortune away besides dumping dust at the front door to be tracked back into the house. Dust should always be swept into the center of the room and picked up in a dust pan. This supposedly gets rid of those evil spirits in the dust. This also applies to sweeping dust from room to room—never do that. It just spreads the evil spirits around.

NOTE: WITH THE advent of women's lib these beliefs about sweeping apply to both women and men. Guys, man your brooms!

◆ Celestial Bodies

Long before astronauts landed on the moon, ancient people were fascinated with the celestial bodies. "Reading" the sky the ancients predicted the future, measured time, and foretold the weather. The ancients venerated the sun, moon, and stars. They believed we should live in harmony with them. It's amazing how often this idea of living in harmony with natural things occurs in the beliefs of ancient peoples. It's a belief we would do well to practice today.

◆

IF YOU'RE SINGLE, look for a shooting star. Spot a shooting star and you will be lucky in love.

◆

THE FIRST TIME you see a new moon, bow to it three times to bring good luck. Don't ever sleep in the light of a full moon. That's bad luck.

◆

IF YOU ALWAYS circle sunwise—clockwise to us moderns—you will have good luck. That's keeping in harmony with nature. A slew of beliefs exist about doing things clockwise—from whipping cream to making bread dough to dancing around the Maypole. I have a friend who washes his car clockwise, and another friend who, when she takes her evening walk, walks clockwise around the block. Ah harmony!

◆

TO THE ANCIENTS, shooting stars were miracles. Besides bringing luck in love, a shooting star was a transfer of souls. One soul left the earth (someone died) and a new soul was leaving heaven and coming to earth to be born. Of course no one in the northern

45

hemisphere seems to have noticed that this soul traffic occurred mostly in August. But if you want to see shooting stars, spend August evenings in the countryside scanning the sky.

———◆———

WISHING ON A new moon goes back to the Egyptians. The reason for bowing to the new moon three times is in honor of the ancient Egyptian Trinity—Osiris (the father), Isis (the mother), and Horus (the son). It's also wise when looking at a new moon to shake any silver coins in your pocket as you make your wish. The moon is made of silver (many folks believe) and the silver coins in your hand are "connected" with the moon. And you thought the moon was made of green cheese!

———◆———

NEVER, NEVER SLEEP in the light of a full moon. You will go crazy. In fact that's where the word lunatic came from—*luna*, meaning moon, *tic*, meaning struck. A crazy person was thus "moonstruck." Even today it's believed Earth creatures act weird when there's a full moon. And of course beware of werewolves and mad dogs who roam in the full moon!

◆ Well-Wishing

Water and women have long been linked in people's beliefs. The association goes: water, tied to the moon, tied to women. Folks actually believed women were under the influence of the moon and water. The moon and water controlled women's moods and fertility. These folks had never heard of PMS! But back to water.

———◆———

WELLS, BEING A source of water, became symbols of fruitfulness. A woman stands by a well and makes a wish. In the ancient tradition, she usually wishes for a husband and children and drops a coin in the well. If she sees her face reflected in the water, her wish is bound to come true. But modern women take note: Wishing for a job promotion also works.

———◆———

THIS IS A difficult superstition to enact these days, wells' being almost inaccessible, but modern folks have adapted the belief to fountains—more prevalent these days than wells, and found inside buildings such as museums and opera houses, and outside in parks.

The fountain at Lincoln Center in New York City for example always has coins on the bottom, cast there by folks dressed in gowns, furs, and tuxedos. Unbeknown to these modern, sophisticated, urban folks, they are enacting a most primitive superstition!

◆ Bones & Wishes

What family doesn't pull a wishbone? This tradition has been carried down by word of mouth through the ages—it rarely even appears in print. But it's an ancient, ancient superstition.

———◆———

TWO PEOPLE MAKE a wish, and each pulls the end of a wishbone. The one who breaks off the larger piece of bone gets his or her wish. Make sure the bone is dry—a day in the sun or on the stove dries it. The bone *must* be from the collarbone of a hen or rooster. I know folks who pull the wishbone of a turkey after their Thanksgiving meal, but turkey collarbones don't work. After all, turkeys are . . . well, turkeys.

———◆———

HENS AND ROOSTERS were mystical to the ancients. The rooster announced the beginning of the day, the hen announced the laying of an egg. These creatures could, it was believed, give folks answers to their problems, as interpreted by diviners and soothsayers. Remember the ancients had problems, too!

———◆———

THE ETRUSCANS, THOSE folks *before* the Romans, even had a hen oracle. This person was often called upon to reveal hidden knowledge. A hen or rooster was killed, the entrails examined—for what, no one can fathom—and the bird's collar bone put in the sun to dry. The wishbone was pulled apart the same as it is today. The Romans stole this custom from the Etruscans and it spread throughout the Roman Empire.

HENS AND ROOSTERS were also used in the practice of alectroyomancy—sort of the same principle as a Ouija board only using the letters of the Greek alphabet and a hen or rooster. A circle drawn on the ground was divided into 24 parts to represent each letter in the Greek alphabet. Grains of corn were put in each section and a cock or hen was led to the circle. The first grain of corn the creature took indicated the first letter of the name of the lady's future husband or, for that matter, the name of the person who stole wheat from the field, or whatever. Then the cock or hen was sacrificed to a special god. The wishbone was removed and snapped in two, by two. I don't recommend this for your kids' next slumber party. Better to give them a Ouija board.

THOUGH CHICKEN IS one of our most common meals today, the Greek Pythagoras in 600 BC advised people not to eat the flesh of the white hen since it was sacred to Zeus. Some folks don't eat any chicken at all. Hindus believe the hen is sacred and do not eat the flesh of hens and roosters, although they do eat the eggs. In fact, the Hindus celebrate the hen in some of the ancient Sanskrit hymns found in the Vedas.

IN THE UNITED States hens and roosters are not celebrated. The raising of chickens is a major industry surrounded by controversy and Frank Perdue. Thousands of chickens are slaughtered daily and we're stuck with our modern day problem of creating yet another new and different chicken dish for supper!

◆ Good Deals—Cards

Unlucky at cards, lucky in love; lucky at cards, unlucky in love. Whatever cards in life were dealt to you, your life is really how and when you play those cards. Here are some tips for good luck.

◆

CARDS ARE A game of chance. We know that today. Mathematicians have even gone so far as to figure out the chances of drawing a full house in a poker game. But back in the 1300s when cards were "discovered" by the Crusaders in the Middle East, folks believed you could change your luck at cards. It's your choice whether you follow this advice when you are in Las Vegas.

◆

WHEN SITTING IN on a card game, get up and twist your chair three times on its forelegs—in the direction of the sun of course, clockwise to us. Or walk around the table three times clockwise.

◆

WHEN PLAYING CARDS, make sure you are wearing at least one garment that is soiled. This could be tricky since most soiled garments smell, and if you smell no one will want to play cards with you.

◆

IF YOU ARE having bad luck in cards you can break that luck by sitting on a handkerchief. Also don't sit with your back to the door. Kit Carson did that. He was shot in the back holding aces and eights.

◆

OTHER CARD TABOOS just make plain sense—don't let anyone stand behind you and look at your cards. Others don't make much sense—the person to take the first pot in a poker game will end up losing for the night.

SOME ARE PLAIN sexist: It is unlucky to play cards (especially poker) in a room where there is a woman. This taboo doesn't say anything about playing poker with a woman—apparently not many women played cards.

HERE IN MAINE women do play cards and always have, according to stories. Folks still talk about Lucy Knox who in the 1700s came from Boston to Maine with her husband (who was known for heroic deeds in the American Revolution) and built a mansion in a little coastal town. The mansion was a bit overdone for tastes in Maine, even then, so many stories are told about these two. Lucy and her husband had eleven children, but only one lived. After her husband choked to death on a chicken bone, leaving Lucy the mistress of a mansion in what was then a wilderness town, Lucy turned to cards. For entertainment she invited all the men in the area to her mansion for dinner and cards. She was the only woman present. That still causes much speculation as to what really went on during those evenings!

Supposedly after a feast, the men and Lucy all retired to the "card room" (not the bedroom) and drank gallons of rum, smoked cigars, and played poker. Lucy was as unlucky in cards as she was in life; she died penniless. "The luck of the draw," folks around here say, glumly looking up to the sky.

◆ Headgear—Kerchief, Hat, & Cap

Kerchiefs are not considered a fashion statement today, but once no "decent" woman went out in public without covering her hair. Today, women have taken off the kerchief—as well as many other pieces of clothing!

◆

WOMEN ORIGINALLY WORE kerchiefs for protection, but not from the weather. Ancients believed women's heads were particularly vulnerable to evil spirits! (No comment.) Supposedly evil spirits always tried to nestle in a woman's hair when she went out of the house. Some folks believed the spirits wanted to get into a woman's hair even when she was at home. This was particularly true of Eastern European cultures. The kerchief was the answer.

◆

THE "SACRED TRIANGLE" shape of the kerchief was the mystical power to ward off these evil spirits. The square from which the kerchief was made represented the four corners of the earth. Folding the square on the diagonal made the sacred triangle and it could be tied neatly under the chin—voilà, a babushka!

◆

WHAT WERE THOSE evil spirits? Nits. Ancient people (women *and* men) were not in the habit of washing their hair. Undoubtedly they had lice!

◆

ARABS EVEN NAMED the evil spirit—Jinn. Jinn, a male evil spirit, was always eager to get in a woman's hair. Men never change! The expression "He gets in my hair," an old Arab saying, has some history to it!

ANCIENTS WERE ACTUALLY baffled by hair on their heads. When it "crackled" that, too, was a sign of evil spirits. They knew nothing of static electricity!

SUPERSTITIONS ABOUT HATS also abound. No one, man or woman, would place a hat on a bed. Evil spirits lived in hats and had wicked tongues. Placing a hat on a bed let those evil spirits escape and tell all the secrets of the hat's owner.

CAPS ALSO WERE the object of superstitions. In fact, those superstitions still exist today—just go to a baseball game. It's common to see team members on the bench wearing their caps backward when their team is losing. Wearing the visor in the back supposedly reverses the team's bad luck. Despite modern improvements in baseball, such as the 90 mile-an-hour pitch, the old cap superstition persists. But it has never worked for the Bo-Sox, however. They haven't won a World Series since 1918! But don't pay attention to the luck of the Bo-Sox, other forces are working there. The next time your son or daughter's little league team is losing, turn your cap around. It just might work!

Part Three

◆

To Have or Have Not— Money

Want to know how to avoid poverty? Try carrying a lucky coin—your coins will multiply. But under no circumstances sew that button on your shirt or blouse while you are wearing it—you will always be poor!

Did you know how your shoes wear out indicates how you spend your money? An anonymous person even wrote a poem about it:

> Wear at the toe,
> Spend as you go.
> Wear at the heel,
> Spend a good deal.
> Wear at the ball,
> Spend all.

Given today's recession this poem might be more helpful than that old ditty: "Early to bed, early to rise, makes a man healthy, wealthy, and wise!"

Money superstitions are not very old as the history of superstitions go. Money has only been around since the tenth century BC. King Croesus was the first person to mint coins. He was a Lydian—from a country located in what we now know as Turkey. Before King Croesus minted his coins, people used salt cakes as currency. Not every country had salt, and salt is a necessity to humans. In fact, the first trade routes in the then-known world developed around trading salt.

Today we have money—the devalued dollar and lower interest rates on your savings. I hope this section is helpful to you in the world of finance.

◆ You Are Due to Get Money if . . .

If your left hand itches you will receive money. It doesn't matter when your left hand itches—whether while watching a basketball game or cooking dinner.

———◆———

SOME FOLKS SAY only if your left *palm* itches, will money come to you. Regardless of whether it's your left hand or your left palm that itches, don't under any circumstances scratch the itch. That will break the enchantment.

———◆———

IF YOU HAVE a scratch on either hand—from the cat or dog or your pet rabbit—that's good luck. It is a sign you will soon receive money.

———◆———

IF YOU HAPPEN to fall downstairs, you soon are going to be rich. This also could mean you will be laid up with a broken leg for some time. So, be careful how you fall. Under no circumstances force this superstition.

———◆———

IF YOU FALL upstairs—which is no easy feat—it is a sign that your credit is rising. I hope this new credit does not carry a nineteen-percent interest rate!

◆ To Get Money ...

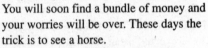

People are always looking for ways to increase their income. Winning the lottery is one way to get money, but the IRS soaks your winnings. There are charms you can enact to bring you a bundle of money, legally tax free.

◆

IF YOU SEE a shooting star, say "money" out loud three times before the star is lost to your sight. You will have some money before the end of the week. Don't waste that falling star you spot on romantic notions! Use it to increase your income.

◆

IF YOU SEE a white horse, put the little finger of your right hand against your chin—just under your lips. Then, spit over your finger.

You will soon find a bundle of money and your worries will be over. These days the trick is to see a horse.

◆

IF YOU PICK up all the pins you find, you will soon have wealth. Of course this goes back to the magic of metal—something primitive people put great stock in. Supposedly magical, the metal would give you wealth. In the old days before currency, this could mean you would have many salt cakes.

IF YOU ALWAYS line your money purse with calfskin, supposedly it will never be empty. Maybe that's why so many change purses, even the cloth ones, have leather liners. I can honestly testify this superstition has never worked for me—but, hey, it might work for you.

IF YOU ARE owed any debts, collect them on Wednesdays. There is no rhyme or reason to this one, but it's worth a try.

WHEN YOU GET new paper money—the kind that sticks together—bite off the corners of each bill. I don't recommend this one, but apparently this is a carry-over from the time when people bit a coin to check that it was real gold. I can't caution you enough, don't bite off the corners of new bills.

IF WHILE MAKING pies you unconsciously trim the crust all around without changing hands, you will be wealthy. The key to this superstition is that you trim the pie crust while holding the pie tin in one hand—without realizing it! If you think about it and purposely do not change hands—this charm won't work. And it doesn't matter what kind of pie it is!

TO BE RICH within the year, eat hog jowls and black-eyed peas on New Year's Day. This is an African-American belief. Some folks say you should eat cabbage on New Year's Day—then you will be wealthy within the year. Other folks say eat fresh parsnips. Be safe, on New Year's Day have all of the above!

◆ You Will Be Poor if . . .

D o you have habits that are destined to keep you financially insecure? Are you always scraping together your pennies and dimes? Here are a few habits to avoid if you want your finances to remain sound.

◆

NEVER EAT BOTH ends of a loaf of bread before you've eaten the middle. If you do, you'll always have trouble making both ends meet in your life. This makes sense. Better to start at one end of the loaf and finish at the opposite end. Besides, if you cut off both ends of a loaf of bread, it will go stale faster. Be prudent!

◆

IF YOU GIVE to the rich, you surely will come to want. This belief also makes sense. Not that the rich aren't needy. In fact the rich are often very needy—in a different way. The rich don't need money, they often need a purpose in life. (This is only an observation since I've never had money.) I guess I'm old-fashioned, and too old to be a yuppie, but there really is truth to that old belief, "a person cannot live for money alone."

◆

IF YOU ARE already broke, have no money in your purse, don't let a new moon shine into it. You will be short of money all month. I'm not sure why people would go around opening their purses to the moon, but anyway, beware.

◆

BY THE SAME token, if you lose your purse, whether it's empty or full, you will be broke for the month. This belief definitely relates to life today. If you lose a full change purse, you will never see the purse, much less the money.

FEW SUPERSTITIONS EXIST around paper money. For one thing, in the Western world paper money is a relatively recent addition—it didn't show up until the 1600s. But you will never be rich if you keep your paper money smoothed out. This makes sense. If your paper money is new and it is kept smoothed out, chances are the bills will stick to each other and when you go to pay for groceries, two twenty-dollar bills stuck together might leave your purse rather than one. Best to wrinkle your paper money.

◆

ONLY A FEW superstitions about money involve women. Not many superstitions exist about women and money because for centuries it was considered "unladylike" for women to handle finances; money was a man's business! Given that belief, you can see why if a wife searched her husband's pockets he would be unlucky in money affairs. Women and money just didn't mix.

◆

DESPITE SOCIETY'S TABOOS, women have always worked for money for as long as money has been around. And some women found a way to earn money at home. Hence the belief that if a woman sews at home between daylight and dark, she will always be poor. Chances are, if a woman finds it necessary to sew from dawn to dusk, she's earning her living by sewing and she *is* poor. "Taking in sewing" was one of the earliest acceptable livelihoods for a woman.

◆

SOME FOLKS CLAIM this superstition has another aspect to it. A woman sewing from morning until evening not only will be poor, but she will also make her husband poor. Frankly, I don't see what her husband has to do with this at all! Whatever ladies, it's best not to sew all day—best to diversify—bake cakes on the side!

◆ The Faces of the Rich

There are ways to read the faces of people to determine if they are rich. These superstitions of reading rich faces revolve around rich men, not rich women. A lady and money were rarely thought of as a twosome. A woman inherited money or married money. Obviously this belief is dated!

———◆———

IF A MAN has a big nose, he is rich. That's one of the cardinal requirements for a "rich face." This description fitted J.P. Morgan to a "T." He had a giant schnozzle. Of course, if J.P. Morgan lived today he probably would have a nose job!

———◆———

IF A MAN has bushy eyebrows, he is rich. I used to think only union leaders had bushy eyebrows—like John L. Lewis, former president of the United Mine Workers.

———◆———

IF A MAN has a mole on his nose it means he is rich. Moles generally mean good luck—unlike warts, which signify bad luck. A mole on a man's nose was a sign of good luck and material wealth. A mole on a woman's nose, or anywhere on her face, meant she was beautiful—but not necessarily wealthy. Of course Liz Taylor has both—beauty (a mole on her face) and money!

◆ Rich Clothes

Y uppies wear clothes with visible labels—from an L.L. Bean to an Oscar de la Renta label. Though label wearing is supposed to indicate status, it doesn't necessarily mean these folks are wealthy. They may simply carry an American Express Gold card!

◆

BE ASSURED, IF you meet a man who wears his hat brim turned up in the back, this man has money—even enough money to lend. Considering men's fashion today, it's important to note that if you meet a man who wears a hat—not a beret or cap, but a fedora—you have met a rare man. Even FBI agents don't wear fedoras today. FBI agents do still wear those trench coats—the ones without a label!

◆

SOME MEN NO longer wear a hat because of the belief that wearing a hat causes baldness. Of course there is no truth to this, but hats have always inspired superstitions. They came in direct contact with the hair on our heads, and hair was a source of mystery, fascination, and superstition to our primitive ancestors.

ODDLY ENOUGH, THE hair on our heads is still fascinating to people today. We shampoo our hair with everything from protein-enriched shampoo to dandruff-fighting shampoo—dandruff flakes being more of our modern evil spirits. We use tons of gel, hair spray, hair conditioner, hair bleach, and dye. We curl, straighten, scissor, and shave the hairs on our heads. And there's no telling if a person has money or not by his or her hairstyle!

ANOTHER BELIEF ABOUT how the rich dress has to do with boots and pant legs. If a man has one pant leg in his boot and one pant leg out of his boot, he has money to lend. It also means he dressed in a hurry, so watch out! He might be a card shark who had to get out of town in a hurry. Better to go to a bank to borrow money—but not an S&L. And if your banker is wearing one pant leg in his (or her) boot and one pant leg out of his (or her) boot—well, better not to borrow the money at all!

WEARING MANY RINGS on your fingers is also supposedly a sign of wealth. In primitive days only leaders of the clan or kings and queens wore rings, rings being a sign of eternal life. But nowadays most people, especially young women, wear many rings on their fingers. There's just no telling who has what these days.

◆ Penny Power

A movement is gaining momentum in this country to do away with pennies. Certain folks, mostly economists, want to eliminate pennies as currency. They find pennies bothersome. These folks advocate rounding off all purchases and bills to the nearest five cents. I find this outrageous. These people know nothing about penny power!

◆

IT'S GOOD LUCK to save pennies in a jar in the kitchen. Any household that does not have a penny jar in the kitchen is bound for trouble and want. A giant empty peanut butter jar is handy for saving pennies, or a glass fruit-juice jar. Whatever jar you choose doesn't matter. It matters that you set aside a jar for penny saving.

◆

ALL PENNIES ARE good to save—the ones that fall to the bottom of your purse, the ones in your jacket pocket, the pennies at the end of the week jingling in your pants pocket. Throw them in that jar in the kitchen.

◆

IT IS ESPECIALLY good luck if you save the pennies you find when cleaning the house—the ones behind the book case or underneath the sofa, the pennies that have fallen behind the cushions on the sofa.

◆

EXTRA GOOD LUCK will come your way if you spot a penny on the ground. Some folks believe the penny must be "heads up," or else it will bring you bad luck. If you find a penny with "tails up" give it away. That transfers any bad luck the penny might hold.

KEEP THE FOUND "heads up" penny in your penny jar—even when you deposit all your other pennies in the bank. The "heads up" penny is a good luck starter and your jar will soon fill with more pennies—economists take note!

◆ Good Luck Coins

lways carry a coin for good luck. Some people have a
special "good luck coin" that they found while walking
with their sweetheart on the day they landed a plum job.
Other folks simply have a lucky coin they've had since
childhood, often it was given to them by a favorite uncle or aunt.
How you chose your lucky coin doesn't really matter; that you chose
a coin to bring you luck does matter.

◆

ANCIENT PEOPLE BELIEVED you should carry a coin with a
hole in it. This brought good luck. A coin with a hole in it is a
throwback to a primitive belief that existed before coins were even
minted. In those days, folks carried a pebble with a hole in it. Such
pebbles are rare. You might find one by combing the ocean shore or
along a riverbank. Because such a pebble is unusual, the ancients
endowed these pebbles with great magic.

This belief about a coin with a hole in it is still very popular.
Convenience stores and drug stores often sell such coins as key
chains. But they don't beat the rabbit-foot key chains in sales—
according to the owner of my local convenience store, that is.

◆

IN THE DAYS of kings and queens, folks believed carrying a coin
with the king's face (or queen's face) on it was especially good luck.
With all the troubles royals have these days (I'm thinking of the
Windsors) I don't recommend following this superstition!

◆ Giving Coins

If you give a wallet or purse as a gift, tuck some money inside. This makes the wallet or purse lucky—these money holders will always have money! Always make sure to put a shiny coin in the purse or wallet. Whether you also drop in a ten-, twenty-, or hundred-dollar bill is up to you.

◆

IF YOU GIVE a garment as a gift, always include a coin with the garment. This makes the garment lucky. Again, a shiny penny is a good coin to give—or a shiny fifty-cent piece. Some folks believe a silver dollar is especially lucky.

◆

NEVER REFUSE A beggar a coin; it can bring bad luck. The beggar will curse you and bring bad luck upon you. This is an ancient superstition. Once it was the custom, when leaving a temple, to give coins to the first beggar you saw. This was especially practiced on the eve of a journey or a wedding. Beggars would stand by temples especially for this reason. Nowadays this can be a difficult custom to practice with so many destitute folks in this country.

◆

ON A HAPPIER note, there's a wonderful old coin custom for couples about to marry. A week before the wedding day, the groom gives his bride-to-be a shiny coin. The day of the wedding, she puts it in her shoe and keeps it in her shoe all day. After the wedding she takes it out and puts the coin in a safe place as the beginnings of a nest egg! Let's hope today he gives her a rare coin—one she can auction at Sotheby's.

◆ Coins and the Dead

A s youngsters, my friends and I believed it was necessary to place coins on the eyes of a dead person to keep her or his eyes closed. We believed no one could pass into heaven with open eyes. Like children around the world, we learned this belief from the older kids.

◆

PLACING A COIN, usually a penny, on each eye of a dead person is as old as the minting of coins. Some folks even placed coins in the mouth of the dead.

The superstition revolves around the beliefs that dead people needed a coin to pay the ferryman, Charon. Charon ferried the dead souls across the mythical river Styx. Styx was the river of hate in Hell. If you got across that river, you entered Heaven.

◆

TODAY, FEW PEOPLE put coins in a corpse's mouth or on the eyes. But often dead people are buried with their favorite possessions—a watch, cuff links, brooch, or necklace. Given the trend of the times, soon we'll start burying our dead with credit cards!

◆ If You Find Money . . .

Who doesn't feel lucky when money is unexpectedly found? It feels like it's manna from heaven. And as of yet you don't have to pay taxes on it! Perhaps that's where the superstition comes from that says if you find money, any amount of money, it is a sign your poverty is coming to an end. This is an easy superstition to believe.

◆

IF YOU'RE LUCKY enough to find money, don't spend it. If you spend it, the good luck deserts you. Best to hold on to that windfall. Invest it carefully and watch it grow.

◆

NEARLY ALL THE superstitions about finding money have to do with coins—not paper money, stocks or bonds, or ATM cards. Paper and plastic currency have simply not been as inspiring to superstitions as coins. This has to do with the fact that coins are metal and certain metals, alchemists take note, bring good luck. Metals have always piqued human imagination. The combination of metals and currency in one is hard to beat for superstitions.

◆

THE BEST MONEY luck to be had is to find a coin on New Year's Day. This means you will have much money all year long. Of course you can't knowingly go looking for money the morning of January 1. If, on the morning of January 1, your husband suddenly gets the urge to remove all the cushions to vacuum the sofa and easy chairs in your house, it's a fair guess he's pushing this superstition, looking for those loose coins behind the cushions. You might mention to him that no superstition works if it is calculated. Then again, you might just let him vacuum the furniture on New Year's Day. That might be an omen that he'll do more housework in the new year.

———◆———

ACCORDING TO ONE U.S. superstition, the best coin to find is a silver dollar. Those are rare coins these days so if you find one, hold it tight.

———◆———

IF YOU FIND a gold coin it's a sign you will have good luck in matrimonial affairs. Better yet, if you find money on your wedding day, you and your partner will be particularly lucky and will never be poor. This is a great superstition!

———◆———

IF YOU FIND a coin with the date of your birth on it, keep it. That coin is your lucky talisman. Of course if you were born in 1947 along with 3.7 million other people—who all have the same lucky talisman—the luck might be spread pretty thin. But superstitions don't keep to statistics, even statistics about the baby boom.

———◆———

IF YOU FIND a coin with the number 13 in the date, it's very unlucky. Throw that coin away. Don't even give it to your worst enemy—you wouldn't wish your worst enemy such bad luck.

———◆———

IF YOU FIND money while on a journey it's a sign you will obtain the "object of your desire"—like a comfortable, quiet hotel room.

———◆———

ANOTHER SUPERSTITION THAT would really work in Arizona or New Mexico has to do with dewless patches of grass. If you see dewless patches of grass in your lawn before sunrise, you can find money there. This superstition never works in Seattle.

—◆—

IF YOU FIND money in the pocket of your winter overcoat when you take it out of storage to wear when the winter winds blow, promises of fortunate business deals are yours all winter. If you send your coat to the cleaners at the end of the previous winter and find money in it when you take it out the following winter, that's an excellent dry cleaner.

—◆—

SOME FOLKS DISAGREE with the overcoat superstition. They claim if you find money in such a manner it's a sign of an impending financial disaster. But that's a coat of a different color, or rather a coat of many colors.

◆ Bad Luck Money Habits

Money can come with bad luck, but take heart; most of the bad luck money superstitions are based on bad actions taken with money. If you are careful, you can avoid that bad luck.

◆

IF YOU BURY money, and never tell anyone and never even draw a treasure map, when you die, you will walk the earth, ghostlike, until someone finds that buried money. This could take decades, especially if you don't leave a treasure map. So don't selfishly keep a secret stash of money buried in the back yard. You'll never again have a good night's sleep, even after you're dead. And you leave a legacy of bad luck to your progeny.

◆

BAD LUCK FOLLOWS a family if a family member dies leaving hidden money. Get your uncle to reveal where he hid his stash. If not, the whole family will suffer.

◆

IT'S A BAD omen to lose your purse, whether empty or full. This superstition is especially relevant today. Even if your purse is empty of money when you lose it, if your address is in that purse—watch out—thieves might ransack your home.

◆

IF YOU FIND money on the ground before breakfast, but there is no wood under it, it will bring bad luck. Better to leave the money there on the ground. Let someone else find it.

◆

IF YOU PICK up your pay check in a bad mood, you will be disappointed in the size of that check. The warning is clear: Don't be in a bad mood on pay day. Don't grumble about all those payroll taxes. Save that for another day. Worse still is if you spend that week's pay in one night—you will lose your job before the end of the month. Be prudent. Hold onto your money and that job. There aren't that many jobs around these days.

IF YOU GAIN wealth unfairly, your descendants will squander it in evil living. The old saying "money got in ill will does not sit still" is based on the belief that if you come by money in ways not on the up and up—watch out. A similar belief about descendants of wealth is: First generation earns the fortune; second generation gets educated with it; third generation squanders it. Earn your wealth fairly or educate your progeny about how to hold onto your money!

IT'S ALSO UNLUCKY to borrow money to pay an obligation. An old saying goes with this superstition. Don't borrow from Peter to pay Paul. So don't borrow on your American Express Gold card to pay off your debts—consider the interest you're paying!

IT'S COMMONLY BELIEVED that it's unlucky for a woman to bail a man out of jail. I think it's unlucky for a woman to have anything to do with a man who lands in jail.

DON'T, UNDER ANY circumstances, let anyone else pick up money you've dropped on the ground. That's for sure bad luck. The person who picks up the money will shortly own the money. Take care of what's yours. Or as folks used to say in the 1800s, mind your own countenance!

Part Four

◆

Good Health Luck

When do you wear cotton socks soaked in vinegar to have good health? Can spinach really give you strength? Why is it bad luck to eat the ends of a loaf of bread? And does a sneeze really mean you're coming down with a cold?

Good health is an asset; an irreplaceable asset. The ancients had all sorts of remedies for good health. Some, we are finding today, had merit—such as the use of garlic, or the brewing of willow bark that is now synthesized into aspirin.

Ancients believed all health remedies could be found in nature —something our scientific world is just beginning to consider. Through trial and error, and intuition, primitive people used herbs, plants, and superstitions to cure their ailments.

How successful are these cures? I advise caution in all matters of health. Always get a second opinion!

◆ Feed A Cold—Starve A Fever

My friend Joe had a cold—sore throat, runny nose, watery eyes, feverish. It was bad enough, he said, for him to stay home from work, lie in bed, and watch soap operas. In fact, he was feeling so poorly the soap operas were "profound." He worried that he would not be well enough to attend the big business meeting at work the next day. It was essential for him to show up. He called his doctor. She prescribed "bed rest, aspirin every four hours, and plenty of liquids." If Joe had pneumonia, she could have cured him with antibiotics. If he had appendicitis, she could have performed an appendectomy. But a cure for the common cold still eludes physicians. And folks still devise home remedies to cure the cold.

◆

"FEED A COLD—starve a fever" is the folk cure for the cold. It's a belief that's been handed down through the ages by word of mouth. If it does appear in medical books, it is disclaimed. But that doesn't stop people from eating soup when they have a cold, and only drinking fruit juice when they have a fever.

◆

ANOTHER FOLK CURE for a cold is never even discussed in medical textbooks. That's a woolen sock. But you must use a *woolen* sock—not a synthetic, "nasty" fiber sock.

The wool sock must be dirty—worn by someone else, preferably someone who is strong and healthy. It's best for a woman with a cold to use a healthy man's soiled sock and vice versa.

The dirty sock should be turned inside-out—the grungy part on the outside. Wrap the sock around your neck. Be sure the foot part of the sock covers the worst sore spot of your throat. Leave it there all night. Be warned—you will smell, and it won't be like Vick's Vapor Rub. Your partner might insist on sleeping on the sofa. But try to get a good night's sleep despite your odor. In the morning, remove the sock and wash! Your sore throat, runny eyes, and fever should be better.

The magic in this cure is the moisture of the dirty sock. The moisture from the healthy person is absorbed while he or she is wearing it. When that same sock is placed on a sore throat, the moisture is "magically" absorbed by the sick person and voilà—the cold is cured.

---◆---

ANOTHER SOCK CURE is to soak clean cotton socks—again, no synthetic fiber—in vinegar. Squeeze out the excess vinegar and put on the socks. Get a good night's sleep. Next morning wash. And best to open the windows and air out the bedroom!

The vinegar in the socks supposedly draws out the fever and cold. Where the cold and fever go is anyone's guess. So be on the safe side, don't hang around folks who wear vinegar-soaked socks.

◆ Teeth and Toothaches

Don't trust people with pointed teeth—regardless of how charming they are! You never know, vampires traditionally have pointed teeth and it's best not to take any chances with a bloodsucker.

------◆------

PEOPLE WITH OBVIOUS spaces between their teeth usually seek success far from their native turf. A similar belief is that people with teeth wide apart will be lucky, wealthy, and widely traveled. This was before orthodontists.

------◆------

PEOPLE WHO HAVE well-placed teeth—no gaps—have fine singing voices. What teeth have to do with singing is anyone's guess.

------◆------

PEOPLE WITH PROTRUDING teeth will live a short life. Of course today kids have braces to correct such things, so it's hard to tell if your partner once had protruding teeth.

------◆------

BREAKING A TOOTH is a sure sign a friend will die. Rest assured there is no scientific basis for this.

------◆------

THOSE OF YOU who have teeth with few cavities have a good deal of sexual strength. If you have teeth susceptible to cavities, you are prone to sexual weakness. No comment.

------◆------

IT'S BAD LUCK to count the teeth of a baby. But if a baby is born with teeth, he or she will be a famous adult—but only if you don't count them!

IT IS BAD luck for a man with false teeth to marry a woman with false teeth. The marriage will be unhappy—but there will be few dental bills.

ANCIENTS HAD A number of talismans to avoid a toothache. Split open a nutshell. Dig out the meat, but be careful to keep the two halves intact. Put a dead spider in one half and close up the shell. Hang it around your neck on a string. You will never have another toothache.

ALWAYS CARRY A wolf's tooth with you. You will never get a toothache. If you follow this belief, don't tell anyone. Chances are likely they won't understand.

LAST BUT NOT least, if you cut your fingernails on a Friday, you will not have a toothache for a month. Note, this does not say anything about toenails!

◆ The Sneeze

Your mother undoubtedly taught you to say "Gesundheit," or "God Bless You," or *something* after you sneezed! Why? If you asked that question when you were a child, you were probably told, "That's what people do. It's polite." What's considered following good manners today is actually exercising a primitive superstition. It's astonishing how many manners started out as superstitions!

PRIMITIVE PEOPLE BELIEVED that by sneezing your body expelled the evil spirits in your soul. Sneezy in the Disney version of *Snow White* apparently was demon ridden! But sneezing could also be dangerous. Your soul (your life's essence) could accidently leave your body with the demons. Hence, a blessing was (and still is) invoked—just in case.

SNEEZING SOMETIMES CAN bring good or bad luck. The Greeks believed if you sneezed to the left, bad luck was in your future. If you turned to the right during a sneeze, you would prosper.

IT'S LUCKY TO sneeze when beginning an argument. This could have been ancient people's idea of "getting the edge" in an argument. If your opposer believes evil spirits escape when you sneeze, you can spook him by sneezing. This would throw him off guard, and you win the argument!

---◆---

GOOD LUCK IS in your future if you sneeze when going to bed. But don't sneeze on your partner. Otherwise, good luck or not, you will not have a partner!

---◆---

IF YOU FEEL a sneeze coming on, but you don't sneeze, watch out! That means you are going to lose someone or something dear to you. These days that could mean a job!

---◆---

THERE ARE SOME "cures" for sneezing. Press your upper lip hard and recite the alphabet backward. No particular alphabet is recommended. The alphabet of your origin will apparently do. Of course, I can't even recite the alphabet backward when I'm not about to sneeze!

---◆---

SQUEEZE THE BRIDGE of your nose. This is nonsense. No known connection exists between the bridge of your nose and the urge to sneeze.

---◆---

YOU CAN STOP a sneeze by pressing on your lip, just below your nostrils. That apparently deactivates the sneeze mechanism.

---◆---

EVERY CULTURE HAS the custom of invoking some god or spirit after a sneeze. The "God Bless You" originated with the Christians. But it's a carry-over from the Romans who took to invoking Jupiter to preserve them every time they sneezed.

---◆---

THE HINDUS SAY "Live." They also vigorously snap the fingers of one hand to scare away the evil beings jumping out of a person who sneezes. The snapping of the fingers prevents those beings from jumping down someone else's throat! If all evil spirits went away with the snap of fingers, what a better world it would be!

82

IN CHINA A sneeze could even affect your ancestors. If you see a friend is about to sneeze, the polite thing to do is clasp your hands and bow solemnly during the sneeze. After the sneeze, you should express the hope that the bones of your friend's ancestors were not rattled by the sneeze.

A ZULU CHILD is taught to say "Grow." To the Zulu, sneezing is a sign of good health. In Persian culture, everyone in the presence of someone who sneezes prays. The Arabs avoid sneezing entirely by washing out their noses with water each evening.

SNEEZES EVEN INSPIRED a rhyme. It matters what day of the week you sneeze.

Sneeze on Monday, sneeze for danger,
Sneeze on Tuesday, kiss a stranger.
Sneeze on Wednesday, receive a letter,
Sneeze on Thursday, receive something better.
Sneeze on Friday, sneeze for sorrow,
Sneeze on Saturday, see your lover tomorrow.
Sneeze on Sunday, your safety seek,
Or the Devil will have you,
The rest of the week.

◆ Yawning—What Happens

Cover your mouth when you yawn." How many times did you hear that when you were a kid? Today it's considered impolite not to cover your mouth. But it all started as a superstition!

◆

EVIL SPIRITS, IT was believed, entered your mouth when you yawned. Those evil spirits caused illness, pain, even death. Trepanning was the countercharm to this bad luck. What's trepanning? If you were possessed by evil spirits from yawning, a hole was cut in the back of your head. This let the evil spirits out! Thank heavens this solution is not sanctioned by the American Medical Association today!

◆

THESE DAYS PEOPLE believe that if you yawn when you are not sleepy, you are bored. This makes sense. After all, most people yawn when politicians talk and while watching a dull movie. And there are plenty of politicians and dull movies! This confirms the old belief that if we yawn when we are not sleepy, we are feeling disappointed.

◆

THE EARLY HINDUS' countercharm to yawning was to snap their fingers three time and repeat the name of a divine power. I don't suggest performing this ritual while in a movie theater; you might be ushered out to the embarrassment of your date.

◆

I RECOMMEND YOU practice what folks did in the Middle Ages. They too believed evil spirits (the Devil) entered the body when a person yawned. They made a subtle sign of the cross in front of their mouths with the thumbs of their right hands. This will not get you thrown out of a movie theater. It might, however, make your date think you are an ascetic.

—◆—

YAWNING IS INFECTIOUS. A fact that must have frightened the ancients when everyone around the cave fire started yawning—lots of evil spirits.

—◆—

IF YOU AND your date yawn together—take care. One of you will be ill. There's some truth to this superstition. If you both yawn through dinner, one of you just might suddenly develop a headache.

—◆—

DESPITE THE FACT that we live in a scientific age, we still don't know for certain why we yawn. Some scientists, (probably on a government grant awarded by those politicians who make us yawn) claim we yawn from a lack of oxygen. Others say we yawn from nervous tension. I doubt the latter. I don't yawn during a political speech because I'm stressed. Rather the opposite. I do cover my mouth—all those evil spirits in that hot air just might enter my mouth. Then I'd be in an awful state!

◆ Hiccoughs

The evil eye causes hiccoughs—it's that simple. If a witch or warlock (people who have the evil eye) gives you the evil eye (looks at you) you get hiccoughs. Of course the hiccoughs might arrive days later—but they can be traced to a curse from the evil eye.

◆

SNEEZING ONCE OR twice is the recommended cure for hiccoughs. This gets rid of the evil demons that somehow entered your body when you were given the evil eye. Sneezing can be induced by tickling your nose with a feather.

◆

OTHER REMEDIES, STILL practiced today, are to hold your breath for a few seconds—this stifles the hiccough demons—and to gargle with a little water—this drowns the demons.

◆

THE CHINESE RECOMMEND swallowing nine gulps of water without taking a breath. Also press the spot on the back of your neck where the neck joins the torso. We know today this has a scientific basis. Applying pressure to the spot puts pressure on the phrenic nerve. This stops the impulse to hiccough. The old superstition is actually true!

◆ Warts

Touch a toad and you will get warts. This superstition is as old as Methusula. So are the ways to get rid of warts. It seems warts have always been considered by humans as ugly. Moles, however, are considered signs of beauty. But let's stick to warts.

◆

RUB GRAIN ON each wart, then feed the grain to the birds. You can also use barley instead of grain. Your warts will disappear within a week!

◆

STEAL A NEIGHBOR'S dishrag. Rub it over your warts. Bury the dishrag by the light of a full moon. I suggest you don't dig up your neighbor's yard to bury the dishrag. Stealing the dishrag is bad enough.

◆

RUB A PIECE of raw beef on every wart on your body. Bury the meat. As the meat rots in the ground, so the warts on your body will disappear. If you're a vegetarian and can't bring yourself to touch beef, take a bean (kidney beans are suggested) and follow the same ritual.

◆

AFTER SEEING A shooting star, pour vinegar on the hinge of a door. Your warts will disappear. If you live in the northern hemisphere, you might have to wait until August before you see a shooting star. This cure of warts has its limitations.

WHEN THE MOON is full, tie a string around each wart on your body. The warts will fall off within a month.

A RATHER GORY cure for warts is to catch a live frog. At midnight take the frog in a box to a nearby graveyard. Kill the frog and rub the carcass on each wart. The wart will disappear within a week.

THIS ONE TAKES time: Touch each wart on your body with the same fingertip the same time every day for a month. The warts will disappear within the next month.

◆ Remember, Remember—Memory

W ant to memorize that report you have to present next week at the sales conference? Stick a copy of the report under your pillow and sleep on it! Somehow magically all the information will filter into your brain! Of course if the report is volumes, it might make for a hard pillow and you might not get any sleep.

---◆---

WANT TO REMEMBER to check the oil in your car next time you get gas? Tie a string around your finger. Be careful not to tie the string so tightly it cuts off circulation; your finger might turn green!

---◆---

DO YOU HAVE a meeting tomorrow with an auditor of the Internal Revenue Service? If so, rub your hands over the head of a bald man. Look over your expense receipts and the checks you wrote. At your meeting you will, with no sweat, remember the details of those expenses you claimed, whether you have receipts or not.

---◆---

IF YOU CARRY a handkerchief, tie a knot in it. That will aid your memory. It's that old belief that if you tie a knot, the knot will hold on to what you want to remember.

---◆---

BEFORE BREAKFAST IS recommended as the best time to memorize that song you agreed to sing at the fund-raiser for the high school basketball team. Supposedly the memory magic is stronger early in the morning.

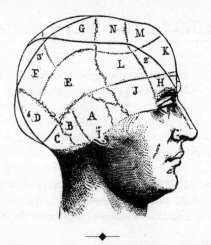

BUT DON'T HANG out in cemeteries reading epitaphs on tombstones if you want to keep your memory. The evil spirits will punish you by stealing your memory. Don't intrude in their space.

◆

TODAY, MOST PEOPLE believe that only folks who can read and write have good memories. This is utter nonsense! Entire national literatures, codes, and sacred books have been handed down from generation to generation by memorization. And these cultures never developed a written language! No prerequisites for a good memory exist—superstitions or not!

◆ An Apple A Day

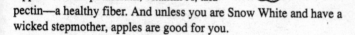

An apple a day keeps the doctor away," goes the saying. Who doesn't like apples? They are delicious and versatile, appropriate with any meal, and they make good snacks. Apples contain potassium, vitamin A, and pectin—a healthy fiber. And unless you are Snow White and have a wicked stepmother, apples are good for you.

◆

THE GREEKS BELIEVED the apple was born in the hand of Aphrodite—the Greek goddess of love. Apples are especially prophetic in matters of love.

◆

WANT TO KNOW if that man in your life loves you? Take an apple and name it after that man. Try to break the apple in two with your hands. Don't use a knife to cut the apple; the magic won't work. If you can break the apple in two, besides being a strong woman, the man you named the apple after loves you.

◆

A SIMPLER CHARM that takes less brute strength combines the alphabet and an apple. While turning the pip of an apple, recite the letters in the alphabet. The letter at which the pip falls off is the first letter of the name of your true love.

◆

APPLE TREES EVEN can predict next year's crop. Many farmers believe that if the sun shines through the apple trees on Christmas day, a good apple crop will grow the next year.

APPLES HAVE BEEN growing on Earth long before they appeared in the book of Genesis. Some historians date the cultivation of the apple back to the Stone Age. That's a million years ago and a lot of applesauce since!

And they continue to grow . . . over 7,000 varieties of apples grow in North America. But Robert Frost has the last words on the abundant apple in his poem "After Apple-Picking Time":

"Ten thousand thousand fruit to touch, Cherish in hand, lift down, and not let fall."

◆ Tea For Many

A slew of superstitions exist about tea—reading tea leaves is just the beginning. If you break a teapot while making tea, you are in for bad luck. This makes sense. Broken crockery always brings bad luck. If you stir tea in a pot, you will have a quarrel with a friend. *Never* stir tea in a pot, regardless of whether or not you want to quarrel with a friend. It's just not done!

◆

A TEA STEM floating in a teapot means a stranger will visit you. May it not be the tax collector! A singing tea pot—one that whistles—means good luck. This also means it's going to rain! Tea drinking stunts the growth of children. This is utter nonsense. Look at Prince Charles—he's tall and healthy, and he grew up on tea!

◆

SOMEWHERE THE BELIEF developed that only tea leaves picked by delicate feminine hands retain a sweet flavor. Consequently, for generations only women were employed to pick tea leaves! Fortunately, no one believes this anymore. Tea harvesting is now an equal-opportunity profession.

Ever wonder why the little round tea cups in a Chinese restaurant do not have handles? It all has to do with the solar circle. The round cups represent one circle. Hold the cups with both hands and you have formed a double solar circle. Sit in a circle while drinking tea from these cups, and you have created the trinity of circles—more powerful than eggdrop soup. The trinity is an ancient and potent symbol for good health of mind and body.

Westerners put handles on the Chinese tea cups around 1550— when they started shipping tea and tea beliefs from China to the rest of the world.

TEA WAS ACTUALLY discovered around 2000 B.C. in China. It was considered a medicine long before it was drunk at social events. Some folks still think it tastes like medicine!

According to legend, the Chinese Emperor Chin-Nung accidently dropped tea leaves into boiling water. He drank the mixture and liked the taste. Shortly thereafter, a cholera epidemic struck China. Chin-Nung ordered everyone to boil drinking water, on penalty of death to those who ignored his decree. Tea leaves were added to the boiled water. It stopped the cholera; the boiled water killed the cholera germs, but in the eyes of the people it was the tea leaves that stopped the cholera. Tea had supernatural power—it became a cure-all for everything! To this day the Chinese call tea "liquid-jade."

TEA IS STILL used to cure colds—although there is no scientific evidence that it does. Wet tea leaves are good for minor burns—the tannin in the leaves is a healing agent and is used in many burn salves.

TEA HAS PLAYED a major role in history—besides the cholera epidemic in China. The American colonists cared so much for tea, and not paying a tax on it, that they revolted and the United States was born. Some folks have strong opinions about tea!

◆ Garlic—The Miracle Plant

G arlic is nature's great protector and is best known as the talisman to the evil eye and vampires. String garlic bulbs together (it's best to use wild garlic bulbs gathered in May) to form a necklace. Wear the necklace while sleeping, working, eating, exercising in the gym, traveling—anywhere and anytime you fear evil and/or vampires might attack you. I don't suggest wearing the necklace in the shower—except if you're staying at the Bates Motel!

◆

IF YOU KEEP a bunch of garlic bulbs on the mantle of your livingroom, only good luck will come your way. It's best to replace the bulbs at least once a month. Don't squeeze or cut the bulbs. Then you'll drive everyone away!

◆

YOU CAN ALSO hang a wreath of garlic bulbs over the door to your home or office. That, too, will protect you. Note, garlic is not a countercharm to CEOs, S&L presidents, lawyers, and tax collectors.

◆

ANCIENT EGYPTIANS WORSHIPPED the garlic bulb as a deity. They also had over twenty garlic-based concoctions to cure everything from headaches to tumors.

◆

HOW AND WHEN the ancients "discovered" the healthful qualities of garlic is lost knowledge. But primitive people were on the right track. Today scientific studies reveal that in some instances garlic is, by consuming huge amounts, effective in lowering some cholesterol levels, lowering blood pressure, and fighting infections. Garlic *is* a wonder.

THE GREEKS AND Romans, including such intellectual heavy-weights as Aristotle, Hippocrates, and Pliny the Elder, considered garlic a cure for many ailments. Greek mid-wives always had garlic around when delivering a baby. Roman soldiers were fed quantities of garlic to give them courage.

PEOPLE TODAY STILL believe garlic wards off disease. I know a man who every day drops a crushed garlic clove into a glass of warm water and drinks it. He just celebrated his ninety-first birthday!

ANOTHER HEALTH HABIT is to carry garlic in your pocket at all times. At least once a week take a bite. This will insure your good health. It might mean, however, that you don't have many friends. Garlic remains on the breath for hours. I suggest you also carry sprigs of parsley—nature's natural mouthwash.

GARLIC ALSO CAN help horses—man's best friend before the automobile. If your horse has lost its appetite, rub garlic on the horse's teeth. Within a week the horse's appetite will be restored.

AND IF YOUR horse recovers enough for you to travel over to the next town by the light of the full moon, take some garlic along. When you come upon a crossroad, stop and plant a garlic bulb in each corner of the crossroad. This will protect you from the evil spirits that attack travelers!

◆ Peeling Away the Onion

Who was the first person to eat an onion? The name of this brave soul is lost in history. But because of the onion's strong taste and odor that lasts and lasts, it got a powerful reputation!

KEEP A PIECE of onion on a shelf in the kitchen and it will absorb any germs that might invade the household. This was often practiced in those cities and town where malaria epidemics occurred. Today we know that mosquitoes cause malaria—and the onion has no power over mosquitoes.

PRIMITIVE PEOPLE EVEN believed onions could scare away the plague and evil spirits. Early Egyptians worshipped the onion. Greeks and Romans consumed large amounts of onions in the belief it increased health. People in the Middle Ages rinsed their hands with onion juice. The juice supposedly killed germs. And you thought onions were only useful to liven up salads!

A PIECE OF onion applied to an insect bite will stop the pain and prevent swelling and infection. Put a piece of onion on a bite and it causes more pain—it stings. That certainly takes your mind off the pain from the bite! No medical evidence exists to suggest the onion fights bacteria or numbs pain.

A PIECE OF onion placed on the back of the neck stops a nose bleed. How this is supposed to work no one knows. In fact, it *doesn't* work. Best to lie flat and put ice on your nose.

TO WARD OFF a cold, cut an onion in two and hang the pieces on a string in your house. Touch the pieces when you walk by. Aside from making your house smell of onions, this practice will not prevent a cold. It's best to take two aspirin, drink fruit juice, and get bed rest.

PERHAPS THE MOST "true" superstition about onions is that if you eat onions at night, you will have insomnia. Indigestion is more accurate! Onions can be rough on a stomach and keep you awake at night. Cooked onions are easier to digest and less likely to cause indigestion. I suggest you eat raw onions at lunch. To be on the safe side eat a piece of parsley afterward. That eliminates onion breath.

ONIONS WERE ALSO used to predict the weather. If the skin of the onion is thick—it will be a cold winter. If the skin is thin—the winter will be mild. I question this wisdom. If stored in a dark, cool storage bin, onions will develop thick skins—and this has nothing to do with winter.

NUTRITIONALLY, ONIONS CONTAIN some potassium, some protein, and a good amount of fiber. It's the onion's versatility that makes it so popular today. It's great raw in salads or cooked in soups, stews, eggs, and with chicken, beef, pork, veal, and lamb— everything but desserts!

◆ The Egg and Us

I n the course of human history, it's likely more eggs have been eaten raw than cooked! Eggs were a chief source of protein for primal humans—and still are in some cultures. In the United States folks often drink raw eggs in eggnog, flavored with a taste of vanilla and doused with whipped cream—a source of protein, but also much cholesterol!

◆

BESIDES BEING A protein source, the egg was the source of all magic. It was the universal symbol of the beginning of life, fertility, and resurrection. Imagine how awed primitive folks must have been when a baby robin pecked its way out of an egg! Even today to watch such a process is awesome.

◆

THE YOLK OF an egg, yellow like the heat-giving sun, had the power to cast out the evil eye. Egg-worshipping cults existed in such disparate geographies as Easter Island and South America. Ancient Egyptians believed the one supreme life was in an egg. This belief is expressed in the hieroglyph for their sun-god Ra—a point in a circle, after the egg.

◆

SUPERSTITIONS ABOUT EGGS are still held, particularly in rural areas. One such belief is that if you see many broken eggs, you will soon have a lawsuit on your hands. And egg on your face?

◆

IF YOU FIND a snake's egg in a hen's nest, your friends are really your enemies. No comment.

IT IS BAD luck to bring a bird's egg into the house. This belief is sound ecological practice. Birds these days have enough environmental ills to contend with just to survive. They don't need folks robbing their nests.

IF A WOMAN dreams of eggs, she will quarrel with her friends. And you thought it meant she was pregnant!

TWO YOLKS IN one egg means good luck for the one who eats them. I know folks who only buy eggs fresh from the farm. Those eggs don't get the factory examination and chances of finding a double-yoked egg are greater.

EGGS LAID ON Friday will cure stomach-aches. Of course only folks who keep laying hens know when eggs are laid. This superstition is simply impossible to follow in urban areas.

WHEN I WAS in college I dated a fellow from Iraq. He was an A+ student at MIT. In his senior year he bought a new car. His family believed that when a new car—or cart—was bought, you had to kill a chicken and pour the blood on it. The chicken's blood would ward off any evil lurking in the vehicle. Living in a college dorm in a Cambridge, Massachusetts, he couldn't follow that practice. But he went to the supermarket and bought a dozen eggs. He put the eggs in the middle of the dormitory parking lot and drove his new car over the eggs. Students at MIT improvise!

◆ The Real Stuff—Bread

I f you're unmarried, never, never take the last piece of bread in the bread basket. You will remain unmarried all your life! Of course if you cook dinner for a prospective partner-for-life and serve Wonder Bread, your chances of getting married are nil!

◆

"BREAD IS THE staff of life," wrote Jonathan Swift. He was not talking about squishy white Wonder Bread. Swift was talking about whole grain bread—the bread eaten by the majority of humans ever since bread was "invented" by the Egyptians. That was around 6000 B.C.

◆

IT'S ONLY BEEN with the advent of refined white flour (in America in the mid-1700s) that bread started losing its nutrients. But nutrients or not, superstitions about bread remain.

◆

DON'T EVER GIVE the heel of a bread loaf to a stranger. You are giving away your good luck. This belief evolved in the Middle Ages—when bread was considered sacred. There is no superstition about feeding the heel to birds in the winter time, however. Just don't give it to strangers!

IF YOU DREAM of a loaf of bread, you will have good luck. But let's hope you don't dream of Wonder Bread; you might have squishy luck.

IF YOU DROP a loaf of bread on the floor, make a wish before picking it up. Your wish will come true. But if you drop a piece of bread, butter side down, on the floor—that portends bad luck. And it's a mess to clean up.

MANY FOLKS STILL believe today that when you "break bread" with someone, that person becomes a friend. This is no longer done literally. Today it's more likely to mean that sharing a meal with someone indicates friendship. Given the sharks I've had lunch with in my lifetime, I prefer not to believe this superstition.

IT'S BAD LUCK to cut off both ends of a loaf of bread. It's also wasteful. The bread will get stale faster. Cutting both ends of a bread loaf is a lot like burning both ends of the candle!

IF A LOAF of bread is upside down on the table, someone in the family will die. But to sailors, an upside down loaf of bread means somewhere on the sea a ship is in distress. Regardless, may your bread always be fresh, whole grain, and right-side-up.

◆ A Pinch of Salt

D o you put the salt shaker on the table first—before the dishes, silverware, and glasses—when setting the table? If so, you're practicing an ancient superstition. And you thought this was the age of logic!

This custom hails from the ancient belief that salt, being a preservative, preserves friendship. The folks who sit at a table where the salt was placed first will be friends forever. That's a nice thought. Let's hope this custom was followed at those high-level S.A.L.T. talks and diplomatic dinners held between Russian states and the U.S.

◆

THE ANCIENT GREEKS even went further with this salt custom. They welcomed folks into their homes by placing a pinch of salt in their guests' right hands—even before offering them a glass of wine. This gesture showed lasting friendship. Odd it was the Greeks who did this; they were, after all, the people who inspired that classic phrase—"Beware of Greeks bearing strange gifts." So be careful following this custom. It's not wise to preserve a friendship with everyone who enters your home, such as the tax assessor.

◆

IF YOUR GRANDMOTHER spills salt she probably throws a pinch of salt over her left shoulder—*without looking over her shoulder*. This is a charm to prevent bad luck that most folks don't practice these days. Salt is so common a staple, we take it for granted. According to the medical profession, we use too much salt in our food. But salt is necessary to sustain life—we all need some salt in our diets. In ancient days salt was precious since it was not always easy to find. Spilling salt meant the worst luck.

SALT WAS ALSO thought to be effective against evil spirits. A small sack of salt was attached to a baby's clothing to protect the baby from evil.

◆

PEOPLE ACTUALLY USED to trade salt ounce for ounce like gold is traded today. The Chinese used coins made of salt. And salt cakes were used as currency in the Middle East. The earliest trade routes were established to transport salt. And as recently as the 1870s when Stanley went into the African bush to find Dr. Livingstone, he didn't take dime-store trinkets to trade for food and information; he took a sack of salt. It worked—in 1871 he came upon Livingstone and the famous phrase "Dr. Livingstone, I presume," was uttered.

◆

BUT BACK TO spilling salt—don't do it. And if you do, do as your grandmother does and don't look over your shoulder when you toss a pinch. Remember Lot's wife in Genesis looked back and she turned into a pillar of salt!

◆ Way Before Popeye—Spinach

Spinach, that leafy green vegetable that your mother and your grandmother tried to make you eat, has inspired superstitions for eons: Eating spinach makes you feel romantic. Eating spinach also calms the nerves. Feeling romantic *is* calming!

◆

SPINACH MAKES YOU strong and helps you to grow. That's the message Popeye has been teaching for decades. But this belief goes back to old King Nebuchadnezzar of Babylon. He lived way back in 600 BC and he ate spinach.

◆

FOR CENTURIES ALL sorts of people have eaten spinach—and oddly, recorded it. King Richard II ate spinach. Samuel Johnson ate spinach. Even medieval monks nibbled spinach during fasts.

◆

HOW AND WHY spinach got such a reputation, we don't know. But spinach is *not* a miracle vegetable.

Spinach does contain vitamin A and C, some potassium, iron, and fiber. It has more protein than most vegetables and it is low in calories.

But spinach also contains oxalic acid. This chemical works in your body to bind minerals—such as calcium and iron. By binding them, oxalic acid makes it impossible for your body to absorb the minerals. Spinach is not bad for you. Spinach just isn't the end-all and be-all of vegetables—regardless of what it does for Popeye.

Part Five

---◆---

Flying & Crawling Good Luck: Birds & Insects

Birds and insects—the two go together. Without birds the planet would be overrun with insects, without insects the planet would have little vegetation and lots of bacteria.

Good and bad superstitions about birds and insects have been around for eons. Early humans lived more ecologically interwoven with nature than we moderns. We spray bugs and poison birds. When Europeans first colonized the American continent they put a bounty on every farm family—a bounty for dead birds. Either farmers killed their quota of birds or they paid a tax. That was bad news for the birds. Today we're a little more respectful of nature, but we've a long way still to go.

My very favorite bird superstition is that if you are awakened by bird song, all will go well that day. That's a superstition I can believe. On summer days in Maine birds start singing around 4:00 A.M. Sometimes I wish they would sleep in, but that's only occasionally. No alarm clock, no clock radio, no timed coffeemaker, can compete with bird song.

A favorite insect superstition of mine concerns the bee. Bees don't work when there's a war! If that's true, bees haven't worked much in the twentieth century! Another one is if a brown butterfly flies into your house, someone in the house will soon marry. Open those windows, ladies!

Most birds and insects are truly international creatures. They make no distinctions between countries. We humans have much to learn from these creatures.

◆ Super-Eagles

Eagles, aloft, can spot prey 1,000 miles away. This is a stretch to believe, but it does explain where the saying "eagle-eyed" came from. Eagles also defy the power of lightning. Eagles are more powerful than a single bullet, more powerful than a locomotive . . . super-eagles. These superstitions may be hard to believe, but how can anyone see an eagle soar and not believe this bird has extraordinary powers? Just its size alone is spectacular. An eagle's average wing span in flight ranges from 6.5 to 8.2 feet.

◆

IN INDIA, UPON sighting an eagle, some take a moment and bow to the mighty eagle spirit—an appropriate show of honor. In the U.S. some folks still believe if you simply spot an eagle resting on a steeple, cliff, or even a skyscraper, success in all your undertakings and great honors will soon be yours. You get all that just from spotting an eagle. That's better than having a Santa Claus in your life. Get out those binoculars!

◆

IF YOU SEE an eagle rise from the ground and soar higher and higher, you will succeed over all the difficulties in your life. That's really the best luck you can have in life! To see an eagle holding a snake in its talons is even better luck. Maybe that explains the U.S. crest. Some folks dislike that the bald eagle is our national bird. Bald eagles can be cowards and can be bested by smaller birds. A flesh eater, bald eagles occasionally are too lazy to capture game and settle for carrion. That is a fact, not a superstition. Bald eagles are a mixed bag of courage, cowardice, industriousness, and laziness—sort of like the national character of the U.S.

109

◆

GIVEN THE EQUIVOCAL nature of the bald eagle, you can understand why the golden eagle is considered the king of birds. (See "Wrens" for the scoop on the battle for the crown). Golden eagles were traditionally the pet of European kings and kept for falconry.

◆

THE UTE INDIANS who live in the U.S. Southwest believe that if you kill a male eagle and eat its heart raw, you will be brave and strong. Many Native Americas believe eagle feathers give one the eagle's sight and courage. But that belief has been held by many people. In fact, Pliny the Elder believed if you put the feather of an eagle in a box with feathers from other birds, the eagle feather would devour the other bird feathers. Eagles were considered superbirds.

◆

THE MYSTERY OF the Eagle's majesty and strength even runs throughout the Bible—in Isaiah is written "They shall mount up with wings as eagles."

◆

BUT PERHAPS SOLOMON really has the final say about the wonderment of eagles in Chapter 30 of Proverbs where he writes:

There be three things which are too wonderful for me,
Yea, four which I know not,
The way of an eagle in the air;
The way of a serpent upon a rock,
The way of a ship in the midst of the sea,
And the way of a man with a maid.

◆ The Hawking Hawk

To keep a hawk from stealing your chickens, put a horseshoe in your fireplace or woodstove. If you have solar heat or an oil furnace, use some ingenuity! A round rock in the fire is also helpful in protecting chickens. The rock magically draws up the hawk's talons so it cannot grab one of your chickens. Ah, magic!

◆

THE HAWK IS a high-powered predator in nature. It has inspired all sorts of superstitions for eons. Unlike eagles, hawks don't eat carrion and they only come around human habitats to hunt something—rodents (the four-legged kind), song birds (the garden variety), and of course chickens. Early humans only saw the hawk hunting, hence its mighty hunter reputation. In the countryside, hawks have been seen as the enemy of chickens for so long that most hawks are called chicken hawks. The correct name of the hawk that hunts barnyard chickens is Cooper's hawk.

◆

LIKE EAGLES, HAWKS seen during a battle mean victory. What I don't understand is if both warring sides see the same hawk—who wins? Regardless of that unanswered question, this belief is worldwide and centuries old. Disparate cultures such as Native American, ancient Greek, and Roman all believed this. And that's one of the good luck superstitions about the hawk. A slew of bad luck beliefs exist as well.

IN INDIA, JUST seeing a hawk means a famine will spread through the land. And if a hawk perches on a house, death is sure to visit.

IF YOU SEE a hawk in the midst of capturing or eating its prey, bad luck is bound to come your way no matter where you live. Many folks say if you don't throw a stone at the hawk when you see it capture its prey, you will have bad luck all your life. For centuries it was up to humans to thwart evil. These days we seem content just to sit around and watch evil on television.

BETTER LUCK IS yours if you see a hawk carry a live chicken away and drop it—and if you recover the chick you'll be very successful in life.

EVEN ARISTOTLE HAD some beliefs about hawks. He thought that hawks captured their prey differently in the summer than in the winter. Hawks supposedly had summer hunting habits and winter hunting habits. He also believed hawks never ate the heart of their victims. There is no truth to either of these beliefs. Hawks hunt the same regardless of the season and they devour their prey down to the bones.

HUMANS HAVE BEEN so impressed with the hawk's hunting talents, they invented falconry. Folks trained hawks to hunt for them—sort of the way some MBA programs train CEO hawks.

◆ Humming Good Luck—Hummingbirds

G ood luck does arrive in small packages. The hummer is the tiniest bird on the planet, and it brings the most good luck. Hummers only live in the Western Hemisphere so all the superstitions about this bird originated in the Americas.

◆

WHEN EUROPEAN IMMIGRANTS arrived in North America they thought the bird "one of the wonders of the Countrey . . . as glorious as a rainebow." Even today, Central and South Americans call hummers "rays of the sun."

◆

GIVEN ALL THESE good feelings and good press it's no wonder superstitions about the hummer are mostly all good. If you do catch a hummer, you will have stupendously great luck. This is, however, more difficult than you might think. Hummingbirds have amazing flying capabilities. They can hover; they can fly backward. In fact, it's generally believed the invention of the helicopter was inspired by watching hummers. Because hummers' wings beat at such a rapid speed they usually appear as a blur to humans. Given all these aerial talents, the hummer isn't easy to catch. If you catch a hummer, your family, your extended family, even the kid who delivers the newspaper to your door, will have great luck. Everything good will happen to all people you are related to, work with, interact with (including those you write to on the Internet) in any way. Hummingbirds bring so much good luck, everyone gets a piece.

◆

BUT REMEMBER, THIS smallest of birds is a feisty warrior beyond its size. It's been known to attack crows and hawks, and it's strong. Many hummers spend the summer in the north and fly to

Bermuda for the winter. That's quite a trip for a bird just a bit larger than a silver dollar.

———◆———

SOME FOLKS BELIEVE that if you catch a live hummingbird you will become wealthy and wear beautiful clothes the color of the bird. Aside from the material wealth you gain, the beautiful colors might be something to strive for. Hummers' colors include blue-throated, buffbellied, and purple.

———◆———

BUT THE ETERNAL question, of course, is *even* given all the good luck a captured hummer brings, what kind of human would want to stifle such a free spirit? My superstition is watch out for anyone who tries to catch a hummer!

———◆———

SOME BAD LUCK is associated with the hummer. If a hummingbird flies into your house and dies, watch out for bad luck. It's generally considered bad luck if any bird flies into your house and dies, but a hummingbird, with its zest for living, brings especially bad luck.

———◆———

UNLIKE MOST BIRDS, hummers don't mate for life. The male courts a female intensely, but does not help build the nest or raise the young. Instead he goes off philandering—a humming rogue!

◆ The Kindness of Robins

Whoever hurts the robin, will spend a life asobbing," is an old saw. Plain and simple, it's a life of bad luck for you if you kill or injure a robin. If you destroy a robin's nest, lightning will strike your house. If you take a robin from its nest, it will bring death to many in your family.

———◆———

MAKE A WISH when you see your first robin in spring. If the robin doesn't fly off before you wish, your wish will come true. But bad luck is yours for the summer if the bird flies off before you wish. So seize the time!

———◆———

IT'S PLAIN UNLUCKY to keep or confine a robin. And if a robin dies in your hand, your hand will shake with palsy thereafter. Beware, robins are a protected species and favorite birds among humankind—especially folks who live in northern climes. Perhaps it's their song, their size, the way they appear in spring after a long winter. Many folks refer to the bird as Robin Goodfellow. And some claim that's why that good guy in Sherwood Forest who stole from the rich to give to the poor was named Robin.

———◆———

ROBINS ALSO PORTEND death. If a robin flies into a church, it's a sign someone in the parish just died. So keep those church windows closed! If a sick person hears a robin sing, he or she is soon to die. If a robin taps three times on a window of a house, watch out—someone in the house will die.

———◆———

ROBINS ARE GENTLE birds, so if by chance you see two robins fighting, prepare for an unpleasant surprise in life.

ACCORDING TO LEGEND, robins generously carried dew in their beaks to refresh sinners who suffered, parched in hell. The scorching heat turned the birds' breasts red—John Whittier wrote:

> He brings cool dew on his little bill,
> And lets it fall on the souls of sin;
> You can see the mark on his redbreast still,
> Of fires that scorch as he drops it in.

Be kind to the kind robin!

◆ The Many Numbered Sparrow

A word of advice: Know sparrow superstitions because sparrows live just about everywhere on the planet—except for maybe Antarctica and the North Pole. In the U.S. you can't avoid sparrows; they live in cities, towns, and countryside. Just smaller than a robin, over fifty different types of sparrows exist. Together all these sparrows make up about one-seventh of the total bird population of the continental U.S.

◆

MANY FOLKS ARE tempted to catch and cage sparrows. A word of advice: Don't do it—the belief is that you will die. If you want to get those flocks of sparrows that live in your backyard to move on, get two cats. Nothing happens to cats who catch sparrows—they are exercising one of the laws of nature.

◆

SPARROWS DO NOT always have a reputation of kindness. According to one Christian legend, a sparrow identified Jesus in the garden when the Roman soldiers appeared to arrest him. But the Hindus see the sparrow in a different light. Kama, the Hindu god of love, is represented in sweetness and light by riding on a sparrow.

◆

IN JAPAN IF you see a sparrow walking on one foot, you will be rich. But that's a rare sighting. Sparrows are active little birds and flit around, rarely landing long enough to walk.

117

IN JUST ABOUT every country where sparrows live it's lucky to see a white sparrow. But that's another rare sighting. If bird watchers here in Maine ever saw a white sparrow, it would make the evening television news. Actually, that would be nice to turn on the evening news and see news of bird sightings rather than the usual people harming people.

IF A SPARROW builds a nest on your house above a window, you will soon take a trip. This could easily happen, sparrows nesting on your house, that is. Sparrows like to nest around people and have for centuries. Maybe that's why sparrows have been around a long time and are considered by many to be rather pesky.

MANY FARMERS HAVE long believed that if they hear a hedge sparrow singing before the grapevine buds, it's a sign the crops will be good. There's no clear cause and effect here, it's nice though that, for once, sparrows bring such good news.

◆ The Good Swallows

In just about every country around the globe, killing swallows brings bad luck. In fact some folks believe whenever a swallow is killed "the sky is cleft with lightning."

◆

IF YOU'RE MEAN by nature and throw a stone at a swallow and injure its wing, one of your arms will be broken within the week. People who stone swallows should get broken arms.

◆

ONLY IN ENGLAND do you find the belief that swallows consort with evil. The story is that every May 1 swallows drink three drops of the devil's blood. Thus if you spoil a swallow's nest, the devil will wreak havoc in your life.

◆

BUT BIRDS ARE usually associated with good spirits, not evil. For a swallow to build a nest on your house is good luck. Since swallows return to their old nests each year (remember the swallows of Capistrano?), you'll have good luck year after year. If one year they don't return, that's a bad omen. The Chinese believe that for swallows to build a nest near your house is a sign of great success for you—especially if they return the next year.

◆

OTHER FOLKS SAY a swallow's building a nest on your house brings poverty. I can't figure out that one, unless they think the real estate value will drop.

◆

SWALLOWS' MIGRATIONS BOGGLED the ancients. Aristotle couldn't figure out where swallows went during the Greek winter and

119

he believed they hibernated in the mud. They did, after all, live in mud houses in the summer.

———◆———

AMONG CHRISTIANS, THE swallow is often called the messenger of life. According to a Christian legend it was the swallow who first spoke that Jesus had died.

———◆———

SOME COUNTRY FOLKS still believe that a treasure is to be found wherever you see the first swallow. This could be difficult since swallows like to sit on telephone and electric wires.

———◆———

PLINY THE ELDER believed the swallow had regenerative powers. He wrote that if young swallows were blinded, their eyes could grow back. Some folks still believe that when you hear a swallow for the first time in spring, you should go to a river and wash out your eyes. That swallow you heard will carry away all your eye trouble. Take note all you who see the speck in your neighbor's eye but don't notice the log in your own eye!

◆ Crow for Crows

Who doesn't recognize the crow? As one naturalist has written, if a person can recognize only four birds, the crow is one of them. Superstitions about the crow are world-wide. The bird is black and the color black has been wrongly linked with sinister deeds in most of history. Unfortunately, the crow takes its lumps.

◆

CROWS CAWING IN the backyard mean death will visit the house. To counter this evil, take off your hat when you hear a crow in the backyard. That's assuming you're wearing a hat.

◆

IF SEVEN CROWS fly in a zigzag line over a house, all the folks living in the house are doomed to bad luck. I asked many people, but no one I asked knew of an antidote to this one.

◆

ACCORDING TO KOREANS if you see a two-headed crow, that's a bad omen. Frankly, if you see a two-headed anything, you have more than a bad luck problem.

◆

THE HINDUS ARE a bit more judicious in their crow superstitions—a crow can mean good luck or bad—depending.

◆

IF A CROW sits on the edge of your roof, that's bad luck, but if it alights in the middle of your roof that's good luck! If the crow lands on the ridge of your house, you will experience a loss. May all the crows in your life always rest on the middle of your roof.

TRAVELING FURTHER EAST, in Japan a crow is good luck. It all started back in 665 B.C. The Emperor was marching with his troops into battle and a crow of supposedly "dazzling brilliance" perched on the point of his bow. The Emperor won the battle and the crow still brings good luck in Japan. It's nice to hear of a good luck superstition lasting.

—◆—

TO FIGURE OUT your future you don't have to go to a palmist. Just take note of the first crow you see in the spring. If the crow is flying, that means you will take a journey. If the crow is cawing something unexpected will happen to you. If the first crow you see is standing on one leg, watch out, back luck will follow. Take heart! How often do you see any bird perched on one leg?

—◆—

GENERALLY, IF ONLY one crow is flying toward you, that's unlucky, but if two crows fly toward you you'll have good luck. If three crows fly toward you good health is yours. If four crows fly toward you, you'll soon be wealthy. Play that lottery number! But if five crows fly toward you sickness is in your future and, worst of all, if six crows fly toward you death is imminent. But in all due respect, if you have nothing to do but stand out in a field counting crows— well, may I suggest you get a job. Or do volunteer work. In the world of superstitions, idleness is also seen as a harbinger of bad luck.

◆ Winsome Wrens

I f you see a wren drop a feather, pick it up. You'll have good luck forever. In the world of superstitions, wrens are sacred birds and bring good luck. When a wren lights on your shoulder, good luck is yours. Sailors believe it's lucky to carry a feather from a wren. "Your ship will ne'er meet storm or tempest." It's even better luck for a sailor if the feather was taken from a wren on New Year's Day!

◆

MOST COUNTRY FOLKS believe the wren is the king of the birds. The legend is that all the birds on the planet assembled to see who could fly the nearest to heaven. The wren, a smart little bird, (the wren is a bit smaller than a robin) perched itself on the back of an eagle. The eagle soared and soared, outdoing all the other birds. When the eagle could fly no higher, the wren flew off the eagle's back and flew even further toward heaven. The wren was crowned king of the birds! Although some folks duly awarded the eagle king.

◆

WITH SUCH A reputation, it's no wonder that if wrens nest in your back yard, you should be good to them. They will bring you great good luck. And they sing a lot!

◆

YOU CAN PREDICT your future according to the direction from which a wren sings. If you're sitting in your backyard on a Saturday afternoon and you hear a wren sing from the west, expect strangers to arrive; if from the southwest, fools will arrive—probably your in-laws? If the wren sings from the north a loved one will arrive, and if from the southeast then religious people will arrive—one of those surprise pastoral calls from your minister, priest, or rabbi. If the wren

123

sings from the south, it means someone you love has been wounded. How? A broken heart or a broken arm? No one seems to know. Best to call all those you love. It's Saturday afternoon, long distance rates are at their lowest. Don't forget to fill the birdfeeder for the wrens.

◆ Owls & Hoots

Owls have inspired a mixed bag of superstitions ever since humans stood up. The ancient Greeks revered owls and believed them sacred to Athena. Affiliated with the goddess of wisdom and learning, the owl was considered wise and gentle. It was a good omen to see and hear the owl. That's probably where we get the "wise as an owl" expression and Winnie the Pooh's gentle owl friend.

◆

SOMEWHERE IN TIME the owl's reputation plummeted and the bird is now an associate of crime, witches, and death. The common barn owl, the screech owl, the great horned owl, all carry the baggage of evil.

◆

OF COURSE IT didn't help the owl's reputation that Roman senators reported hearing an owl in the senate chamber just before Caesar was stabbed. Anyway, to this day people around the planet believe when they hear an owl hoot, someone close to them will shortly die. Some Native Americans believe the owl is not even a real bird; it is the spirit of the dead warning of yet another death to come.

◆

TO COUNTER THIS evil owl power—put irons in your fire. Or throw salt, pepper, and vinegar on the fire—the owl will get a sore tongue, hoot no more, and no one close to you will die. That's very good luck.

◆

OTHER FOLKS TIE a knot whenever they hear an owl hoot. Better yet, some people recommend taking off your clothes, turning them inside out, and putting them back on. You might not want to do this if you're out in public.

IF YOU'RE ON the way to visit the one you love and you hear an owl hoot, your lover will prove to be false and your romance will end. So keep your car windows up and the radio blaring so you won't hear that hoot. And don't mimic an owl's hoot—the clothing on your back will incinerate. That's a powerful evil bird! Well, imitators are boring adults.

ROMAN MEN BELIEVED that if the heart of a horned-owl was put on the left breast of a woman while she slept, she would reveal all her secrets! Of course women to this day know differently. Nothing makes a woman reveal all her secrets, unless of course she's a woman like Madonna who does seem, repeatedly, to reveal *all* her secrets of heart and flesh.

PLINY THE ELDER is responsible for labeling the owl as evil in print. He wrote that the owl "always betokeneth some heavie newes, and is most execrable and accursed." This one man's verdict has stuck for centuries.

ONLY THE WHITE owl—the snowy owl—is good. To see a white owl during the day means good luck, prosperity, and ease will shortly be yours. No wonder the snowy owl is protected by the EPA!

ALL OWLS ARE neat birds. Without them, the planet would be overrun with rodents. Just because owls sleep by day and fly by night is no reason to despise them—ever notice how people are suspicious of folks who are "night owls"? But then perhaps owls have survived because they are nocturnal. People simply are too tired to wait up for an owl to appear so they can kill it.

126

AND THERE'S ONE owl superstition that's good—good for women that is. Some folks to this day believe that any man who eats roasted owl will be obedient and a slave to his wife. Wives, get out the roasting pans!

◆ Butterflies & Luck

A h the butterfly—whatever you do, don't harm a butterfly. Butterflies are free-spirited beauties, a gift from nature of color, energy, and whimsy. Besides, on the practical side, butterflies are very important to a balanced Earth ecology.

◆

TO SEE A white butterfly means good news to you. But if you collect butterflies (regardless of their color), kill them, and stick pins in them you will die an unnatural death. I'm not sure about the "dying an unnatural death," but I'd think twice before becoming a collector of butterflies.

◆

SAM, A FRIEND of mine, was an avid butterfly collector—one of those guys who spent his summer weekends capturing butterflies, sticking pins in them, and mounting them in show cases. While he pursued this supposedly harmless hobby, his life went from bad to worse. His marriage broke up and he lost his job. Then, during a nor'easter, a tree in his yard fell onto his house, caving in the roof over his den where he kept his butterfly collection. His collection was destroyed. Sam decided he had to change his life, change his attitude. He gave up butterfly collecting, spent his weekends repairing his house and his life. Well he soon got a job—a better one than he had— and he and his wife reconciled.

The key was probably in changing his attitude—after all, what kind of man (and butterfly collectors are mostly men) would want to stick pins in such a beautiful, free creature like the butterfly?

THE CHINESE BELIEVE it's bad luck to catch butterflies because they are departed spirits who have returned to check out what's happening on earth. If that's the case, they don't stick around long; butterflies only live for one or two weeks.

OTHER SUPERSTITIONS ABOUT the butterfly have to do with their colors. If the first butterfly of the year you see is white, you will eat only white bread all year—no whole wheat bread for you! If it's brown, you will eat brown bread. This belief requires quite a stretch.

IF YOU'RE PLAYING poker and a butterfly lights on your hand, you will win the poker game. Rarely does this happen. Butterflies for the most part stay away from people and they don't fly at night. Moths do. But if you and your friends happen to be playing a game of poker in the garden in the middle of a summer afternoon, a butterfly might light on your hand—if so, up the ante.

IF A BUTTERFLY lights on your head—whether you're playing poker or not—it's an omen you will hear news from far away. Yes, people believed this before the Internet existed.

◆ Ladybug, Ladybug, Fly Away Home ...

Never, never kill a ladybug. You will have really bad luck if you do. Also you will kill one of nature's necessary creatures. Ladybugs devour aphids, a common garden and houseplant pest. Ladybugs are our valuable allies!

◆

JUST TO SEE a ladybug brings you good luck. If the ladybug lands on you, joy joy—all your aches and pains will fly away with the ladybug. If you are a single woman and the ladybug lands on you, then flies off, note what direction it flies. That is the direction from which your future husband will arrive.

◆

LADYBUGS ALSO CAN tell you whether you will go to heaven or hell when you die—that is, if you are interested in knowing such a thing. But folks believe that when a ladybug lights on your hand and you ask it: "Where will I go?", you'll have your answer when it flies away. If the ladybug flies up—you go to heaven. If it flies downward—you go to hell. Ah, if only it all were so simple!

◆

COUNTRY FOLKS BELIEVE that if the number of spots on the wings of a ladybug exceed seven it is a sign of a poor harvest. If fewer than seven spots are on the wings, it will be a good harvest. This superstition almost guarantees a good harvest; multi-spotted ladybugs are rare ladies!

◆

ANCIENTS BELIEVED LADYBUGS came to earth in flashes of lightning. Ladybugs were even sacred to the Norse god of love and beauty, Freya. So be kind to ladybugs.

◆ Bees, Hornets, & Wasps

It's unlucky to kill a bee. Granted, it's tempting when a bee is buzzing around you, but don't do it. You'll bring down bad luck on yourself as sure as the moon shines. But if you do kill a bee, keep the dead bug in your purse or wallet. This will bring you wealth. You might have bad luck, but at least you'll have money. Bad luck *and* poverty are to be strenuously avoided.

◆

ALTHOUGH MANY TODAY believe bee stings cure arthritis, nothing has ever been scientifically proven. And if a bee does sting you, aside from having to nurse the sting, bad luck and losses will darken your door.

◆

IF A BEE stings you, rub grass on the sting—breathe on the grass while you are rubbing the bee sting. This *might* turn your fortune around.

◆

IF YOU'RE OUT for a walk and have nothing else to do, and you follow a bee to its nest, but don't disturb the nest, you will have good news—probably about a honey of a deal!

◆

IF A BEE flies in your window, don't panic and reach for the bug spray. It means you will hear good news—good news has strange messengers.

SWARMS OF BEES are no different. Except for the Romans who believed seeing a swarm of bees was a bad omen, most people believed a swarm of bees meant good luck, wealth, and success, no matter what continent they and the bees inhabited.

◆

WHEN THE SWARM settles—that's a different story! Folks in Wales believe when bees settle on the ground, someone will die. And if a swarm lights on a tree branch in your yard—you soon will die! Killer bees—even in Wales.

◆

WHERE BEES NEST is yet another story. If bees nest under the eaves of your house—none of your daughters will marry.

◆

HORNETS AND WASPS nesting on your house means something else entirely. Hornets bring good luck. When wasps decide to live in your house, however, it's a sign you're a spendthrift and you'll come to want. Apparently even insect wasps don't like ostentatiousness!

◆

IT'S A MIXED bag about killing hornets. If you kill the first hornet you see in the season—that's unlucky—but in England killing the first hornet you see brings good luck. Likewise if you kill a wasp in the early spring, you will conquer all your enemies and have good luck for the year. Just this once it might be wise to defer to the English.

◆

WE'VE COME A long way regarding bees, hornets, and wasps. Pliny the Elder believed that to cure a fever you should catch a wasp with your left hand, kill it, and attach the dead bug to the patient's chin. Thank the lucky stars for Tylenol!

◆ Chirping Crickets

Primitive folks believed crickets were on earth to teach mortals to be cheery! So don't ever kill a cricket. Why would anyone ever want to kill a cricket? Remember Jiminy Cricket in Disney's *Pinocchio*? A most happy fella!

◆

GREEKS WORE CRICKET amulets to protect them from all evil. Cricket amulets aren't exactly a fashion statement today, but many kids catch crickets and keep them as pets.

◆

IF A CRICKET leaves a house—bad luck arrives. So keep your cricket content.

◆

BEWARE OF STRANGE crickets. If suddenly you realize the cricket chirps are "different," prepare for bad luck. Unfortunately I don't have any tips on identifying "strange" crickets. You'll just have to listen hard for a different chirp.

◆

COUNTRY FOLKS BELIEVE crickets live to be hundreds of years old and could tell us the history of the world—this history being passed down, from cricket to cricket. The catch is we don't know how to understand the cricket when he chirps. And it is he who chirps—not she. Actually the chirping is caused by his rubbing his wings together.

◆

IF YOU SEE a white cricket, that's a sign your absent love will return. But don't wait around hoping to see a white cricket. They are very rare and you could be a hundred and two before you saw one. It's better to find a new love.

133

SOME FOLKS BELIEVE a cricket will eat holes only in the clothes of folks who kill their mates. This, of course, is nonsense. Crickets, if they settle in your woolen drawer for the winter, will eat their way through your woolen socks and sweaters, regardless of whether or not you've committed homicide.

◆ Itsy, Bitsy Spiders

Want to have good luck always and never want for anything? Carry a spider web in your pocket. How you can do this without the web becoming a sticky glob, I don't know. Spider webs are one of those natural, delicate, beautiful things, that we, in our clumsy human way, destroy when we touch them.

—◆—

SPIDERS AND THEIR webs have received more than their share of superstitions ranging from curing fevers, to predicting the future. If you have a fever, swallow a spider with some syrup. The spider will eat up the fever. Although this is an old belief, I recommend *not* doing this!

—◆—

TO ENSURE NEVER catching a fever, wear a dead spider in a nut shell around your neck. No scientific basis exists for this belief. And if you tell your friends this, they will probably think you're nuts!

—◆—

IF YOU ARE sitting in your living room and a spider crawls across the floor toward you, you will soon have a quarrel with a loved one. You probably will quarrel over whose turn it is to clean the house! But don't kill the spider. Capture it and free it outside. It's bad luck to kill spiders.

—◆—

SPIDERS HAVE EVEN inspired a poem—often recited by kids.

> See a spider in the morning,
> It is a warning.
> See a spider at noon,

It brings good news.
See a spider at night
It brings joy and delight.

◆

IF WHILE WATCHING a spider weave a web the spider drops a single thread, then turns upward, you will have good news. But if the spider turns downward, you will have bad news. Of course whether the spider ascends or descends all depends on how tired it is!

◆

ONCE THE WEB is woven, if you run into it accidently, expect to soon run into a friend. Let's hope your friend is not in the spider web!

◆

IF YOU WALK through a spider web, you will soon receive a letter with good news. Of course, you cannot deliberately run or walk into a spider web. The charms won't work. Note: It's bad luck to force any superstition!

◆

CHARLOTTE, A MOST capable spider, once befriended a pig named Wilbur. Wilbur's life was in danger. Charlotte was not only a skilled weaver, but succinct in her choice of words. She wove those words into her webs. She saved Wilbur from the slaughter house. That's one empowered spider!

◆ Antsy Ants

Y ou might find this one hard to believe, but if ants thrive in your backyard, you'll be wealthy. Better yet—if you say "mumblyup" over an ant hole it will bring all the ants to the surface. Why anyone would want the ants to surface mystifies me; however, if the need should arise, this is the solution.

◆

IT'S BAD LUCK to kill ants and if you step on an ant hole, it will rain.

◆

WHAT HAPPENS TO you if you kill ants? Are you sure you want to know? People used to believe that if you kill ants, when you die they will run over your dead body before anyone has a chance to bury you. Despite their tiny size, ants seem to inspire horror in people. In modern days we created giant ants—remember the movie *Them*?

◆

NATURALIST EDWIN WAY TEALE claims ants are very much like humans. They go to war, and supposedly some types of ants march in columns and attack in unison. In fact, according to some folks, if you see an ant war, that means you soon will go to war.

◆

TEALE ALSO POINTS out that sometimes tropical ants live in cities—nests that contain nearly half a million ants. That's a creepy image. Ants also have intricate living patterns. They keep "cattle"—smaller insects from which ants get honeydew by a kind of milking. Ants plant fungus gardens and gather crops. Some ants harvest grain and store it in granaries they build in their nests. Ants have a hierarchical society—ranging from the queen ant to lowly workers who never leave the nest. It's scary to think such minute creatures are so organized. But take heart—if you are stung by an ant, the superstition is you'll soon be very prosperous. You won't even think about ant societies!

———◆———

ANTS HAVE, HOWEVER, always scared people. Some farmers believe if they kill ants, the ants will bewitch the cows and prevent them from giving milk. These little creatures are cunning!

———◆———

IN INDIA WHEREVER red ants colonize is a sign of wealth. Generally speaking, though, around the world black ants are good luck; red ants are bad luck.

———◆———

BUT IN THE West Indies if you see a procession of ants, regardless of their color, supposedly you'll soon be going to a funeral! Beware, power comes in the smallest of sizes!

Part Six

◆

Lucky Blossoms: Lucky Trees

The Greeks believed that flowers on the table prevented dinner guests from getting drunk on the wine served. Ah, if it were only true!

The bread will sour if you bring flowers in from the cornfield is another early belief. Actually this is ecologically sound. If our forebears picked flowers the way folks do today, we wouldn't have any flowers to pick.

Someone is deeply in love with you if the flowers you wear wither in a short time. Any idea who? Another superstition is that people who wear flowers with the stems pointing upward are in love. Actually if someone did wear a flower on his or her lapel upside down, folks would wonder . . .

My favorite tree superstition is that when you plant a tree, hold the tree with both hands while a friend stands by you. The tree will flourish.

To cut down a green tree is very bad luck. This is another ecologically sound belief. Trees are an important link to Earth's ecological balance.

Hindus, Greeks, and Buddhists all thought, and some perhaps still think, it's a great sin to cut down a tree. In ancient Persia just to plant a tree brought you good luck.

Superstitions about flowers and trees are perhaps the oldest beliefs of which we have an oral and written record. From primitive humans through today, trees and flowers have been an intricate force in our symbolic thinking. And since trees were sturdy, leafed out every spring, or, in the case of evergreens, stayed green all year long, trees were gods and goddesses. Flowers bloomed every year, had beautiful colors and smells and, hence, were magical. Let's face it, our ancestors had much better respect for trees and flowers than we do.

◆ Lover's Hope—Mistletoe

Mistletoe is a good excuse to kiss that person (unannounced) you've always wanted to kiss. But be careful. I'm not sure if kissing under the mistletoe now falls into the category of sexual harassment—of women or men. It's getting that person *under* the mistletoe that's the trick.

◆

MISTLETOE AND LOVE, mistletoe and good luck, mistletoe and good health are all beliefs as old as the hills.

◆

WILL YOUR SIGNIFICANT other ever marry you? Mistletoe leaves can tell you. Draw a circle in front of the fire. Take two leaves of mistletoe. Give one your name and place it in the circle. Name the other with your lover's name and place it outside the circle. If your lover is to marry you, the lover's leaf will jump inside the circle next to your leaf. I've never heard of jumping mistletoe leaves, but, hey, if beans can jump, mistletoe leaves can jump.

◆

DO YOU HAVE a bad case of the hectics? Stressed out, too much to do, not enough time? Every March, in the full moon, cut mistletoe and make a small wreath. Hang the wreath in your living room all year. Mistletoe woven into a circle cures the hectics. If you don't know what the hectics are, you are a rare person of the late twentieth century. And if you're a man who doesn't know what the hectics are—ask any woman.

◆

GENERALLY, MISTLETOE IS supposed to ward off sicknesses. It can cure all poisons. But it has to be cut off the oak tree with a golden hook and not touch the earth. If that happens, watch out for disasters to occur.

MISTLETOE WAS ALWAYS gathered for the Celtic winter solstice festivals. The arch-Druid (the head honcho of the Druids) cut it off the oaks with a golden hook or sickle. Besides an antidote to poisons, it was used as a charm against those innumerable evil spirits. Mistletoe was also supposed to encourage fertility.

IN AUSTRIA IT'S reported some folks believe if you lay mistletoe at your bedroom door, you'll have a sweet sleep and beautiful dreams. That should cure the hectics and encourage fertility!

MISTLETOE IS ALSO effective with cattle. If you give a bough of mistletoe to the cow that calved first after New Year's Day, you prevent bad luck from attacking your entire dairy. Protect your cows—give them mistletoe. Don't worry; you don't have to kiss them.

IF IN NOVEMBER/DECEMBER no mistletoe can be found on oak trees—watch out. Great danger is at hand. Nothing can be done if you don't find fresh mistletoe. Last year's mistletoe no longer possesses the magical charm. May you always find mighty oaks where mistletoe grows.

◆ The Useful Dandelion

There's no excuse for not being able to recognize a dandelion. Dandelions grow not only in city parks, but between cracks in sidewalks around the world and in suburban and country lawns no matter how well-kept or unkempt.

◆

SINCE DANDELIONS HAVE been around forever, folks have a lot of beliefs about the flower—other than the fact that the first spring dandelion roots are good to eat.

◆

IF THE BLOSSOM of a dandelion blows in your face, you will soon receive a letter of important business. It doesn't matter if the letter arrives via the Internet, a fax, Federal Express, or the outdated U.S. Postal Service. It is *the letter you've been waiting for all your life*—that letter from Publishers' Clearing House with the winning ten million dollar number.

◆

IF YOU'VE EVER wondered how long you will live—"Will I or won't I make age 60?"—pick a dandelion with those white fuzzy seeds—dandelion puffs we kids called them. Blow on it until all the seeds are dispersed. Count the number of times you blew on it. That's the number of years you will live. But it's not such a good idea to do this. You don't need any more stress and life is easier not knowing at what age you're going to keel over. It's better to use the dandelion puffs to find out what time of day it is. To do that, pick a dandelion puff. Blow on the puff three times. The number of seeds left tells you what time it is. Take note: The puff does not distinguish between Eastern Standard Time, Daylight Savings Time, Central Time, or

Pacific Time. This particular way of telling time is eons away from digital clocks.

◆

KEEP THE FIRST dandelion that grows in your garden. The belief is that if you don't dig up that dandelion you will have a blooming garden that summer. In its proper place the dandelion is a good luck flower, not a weed! If the dandelion puff flies apart when there's no wind, grab your slicker. It will soon rain.

◆

BACK IN VICTORIAN days, when communication between the sexes was even more vague than it is today, one Lady Mary Wortley Montagu wrote a book on flower language. People didn't have to communicate in words. As Lady Montagu wrote, there is no "flower, no weed that has not a verse belonging to it; and you may quarrel, reproach, or send letters of passion, friendship, or civility, or even of news, without even inking your fingers." Well, the Language of Flowers would save on the fax bills, but deplete the flower garden. Fortunately, today we have Deborah Tannen's books and we at least *try* to speak more clearly to members of the opposite sex. For what it's worth, however, in *The Language of Flowers* the dandelion was supposed to communicate "rustic."

◆ The Undefeatable Snowdrop

Do you want pure thoughts? Pin a snowdrop on your sweater. If you wear a snowdrop it's supposed to insure the purity of your thoughts! You might also consider giving a snowdrop corsage to friends whose thoughts you deem less than "pure." Of course you all might be out of step with the late twentieth century since no one seems to care about purity these days.

◆

WHEN IT'S SNOWING on the first day of spring and you spot a snowdrop—there in a protected, sunny nook, your first reaction is to pick the flower and bring it inside to add a touch of spring to the house. Be warned that many folks believe bad luck will result from bringing the snowdrop inside. Some folks even say they bring death—something about their look that resembles a corpse in a shroud. I don't buy into this superstition. A beautiful, harmless flower such as the snowdrop can't possibly bring you bad luck.

◆

IF YOU EAT the first snowdrop you find in the spring, you won't tan in the summer! I don't know many people who go around eating spring flowers, but if you want that gorgeous tan to impress your significant other, don't eat a snowdrop. Christians believe the snowdrop always blossoms on Candlemas day—February 2. Perhaps in the Middle East snowdrops blossom on February 2, but in Maine we usually have so much snow there aren't many protected sunny nooks. But hope springs eternal, and I still look for signs of spring by searching for a snowdrop in February. By the way, in *The Language of Flowers*, giving snowdrops to someone means you're giving that person hope—a rare gift in the time of snow and ice.

◆ The Innocent Daisy

Want to be the life of the party? Whoever picks the first daisy of the spring becomes possessed with a spirit of flirtatiousness beyond control. Just make sure it's a safe party you're going to. Appoint a designated driver. The penalty for driving under the influence of a daisy is stiff.

—◆—

IF YOU DRINK a concoction of boiled daisy roots you will shrink—that's what happened to Alice when she tripped into Wonderland. You won't, however, meet a vested white rabbit or play croquet with the Queen of Hearts, but you will diminish in size. If you have any small doors to go through in life you might consider a drink made of boiled daisy roots.

—◆—

IT IS UNLUCKY to transplant wild daisies to your cultivated garden. Such hardy free spirits don't get along with all those cultivated lovelies.

—◆—

OF COURSE THE age-old answer to whether he loves me or loves me not, or she loves me or loves me not, can still be answered by daisy petals. But whatever you do, make sure you don't pick a horse daisy to answer this burning question. What's a horse daisy look like? No ones seems to know. But I thought I should warn you. If you handle a horse daisy you will get warts.

—◆—

IN *THE LANGUAGE* *of Flowers* the daisy means "innocence." Apparently the Victorians never heard what happens to you if you pick the first daisy of spring. Can one flirt and remain innocent? Another life question to ponder!

146

◆ The Persevering Daffodil

I t's very tempting to pick those early blooming daffodils and put them on the kitchen table to gaze at, sleepy-eyed, over your first cup of morning coffee—but don't. It's very bad luck; it can mean a visit from the Grim Reaper.

◆

THE DAFFODIL REALLY is a "Mary Sunshine." Before spring arrives, when ice storms and frosty mornings are the norm, the daffodil blooms yellow, bright, and cheery. That's some optimism!

◆

BUT BE WARNED; if you insist on picking the daffodils and bringing them into your house, no ducklings will hatch that spring. This daffodil stuff is serious business. So keep your life *and* your ducks in a row, and forget about picking the first daffodils you see in early spring.

◆

IF YOU BRING any daffodil into the house, even if it's a late bloomer, and your goose is sitting by the wood stove, those eggs, too, won't hatch. How daffodils affect duck and goose eggs *is* puzzling.

◆

OF COURSE NOT everyone believes daffodils in a house bring bad luck. Some folks believe the daffodil is good luck—in the house or not. To them the daffodil is a flower beloved by God and it forever blooms in the Garden of Eden. It's supposed to be good luck to pick the daffodil and wear it over your heart. Ultimately, whether to house daffodils or not to house daffodils is your choice. I say don't be daft, leave the daffodils outside. Whatever you choose, good luck to you, and may all your duck and goose eggs hatch.

◆ Violets Don't Shrink

Don't be misled by the term "shrinking violets." Violets bring good luck. Why violets have been considered shy is lost knowledge, but if you want gook luck, I suggest you change your attitude about violets.

◆

IF YOU DREAM of violets, you will have good luck. And if you gather the first violets in the spring, your deepest wish will come true. Simply picking violets any time of their season means you will have great success in all your endeavors. So don't shy away from violets. Get out there and start gathering.

◆

BESIDES THESE PLEASANTRIES, violets have a practical side. Apply violet leaves to any wound, and the evil spirits causing the wound flee. Voilà, the wound heals. Be sure to wash the leaves first. You don't want to use leaves infested with minute insects.

◆

A GARLAND OF violets worn around the head curses headaches and dizziness. This is supposed to be better than Extra Strength Excedrin. It might be awkward, though, wearing a garland of violets in the office to cure that headache the treasurer's report gave you.

◆

VIOLETS BOILED IN oil will cure sore eyes. I'd pass on this one. You will too when you think about it—would you really put a paste of violet leaves and boiled Mazola on your eyes? Better to visit an ophthalmologist.

◆

VIOLETS WERE THE flowers of medieval minstrels. In Toulouse, France, during the twelfth century, the poetical contest prize for the

best poem recited—not read, that's a big difference—was a coveted, carved-in-gold violet. For the winning bard, the violet usually meant a plum job in some royal court.

———◆———

GOLD VIOLETS OR not, mind your violets. There's nothing shrinking about them. And remember, they're perennials—they bloom year after year after blooming year . . .

◆ Hi Lily, Hi Low

T oo bad the folks who lived in the house of Usher didn't think to bring in some lilies. The Chinese believe that as long as there is a lily in the house, no evil will live there. Quick, call FTD and order a bunch of lilies to be sent to the U.S. Congress!

———◆———

IF YOU FIND the first white lily of the season you will have great strength. The first lily is supposed to give strength beyond that which you can get from lifting weights. Watch out Arnold Schwarzenegger. If the justice system fails, as often it does, and an innocent person is executed, three yellow lilies will grow on his or her grave.

———◆———

REGARDING JUSTICE—DO you want to find the clue that breaks the Jimmy Hoffa mystery? Take old leather and plant it near a bed of lilies. You will soon be given a clue to any crime committed in the past. Be careful; you might end up with a ton of clues.

———◆———

LILIES ARE ALSO associated with trouble. Some folks believe if the lilies in your garden bloom all summer, your family will have great trouble in the winter. Actually this superstition probably springs from sour grapes—a jealous neighbor whose lilies didn't bloom all summer while yours did.

WANT TO LEARN whether or not your lover is faithful? Plant an Easter lily bulb. Place a small piece of paper with your lover's name on it with the bulb. How high the lily grows indicates how faithful your lover is.

DON'T KNOW WHAT to give your step uncle's seventeen-year-old daughter who just eloped? If you give a potted lily to a bride she will grow strong, vigorous, resist temptation, and be chaste throughout her married life. Given that, she just might appreciate luxurious silk sheets more.

IN THE OLD Testament Judith was crowned with lilies, as the belief was that lily flowers counteract the power of enchantment. The lily was the emblem of many chief goddesses in ancient Greece, Crete, and Rome. According to an ancient Semitic legend the lily sprang from the tears of Eve when she learned she was ousted from the garden and was "with child." What woman wouldn't cry after learning she was pregnant and being kicked out of her home?

◆ The Sacred Oak

Just about everywhere the oak is indigenous, it has been revered. To cut down an oak is fatal—to the oak *and* to you. It's especially unlucky to fell an oak that bears mistletoe. If you happen to be so foolish as to cut an oak bearing mistletoe, at least try to rectify your error. It's suggested that you leave some of the mistletoe on the tree stump to sprout again. Mistletoe hope springs eternal!

EVEN TODAY, SOME country folks suggest that for good luck's sake when someone in your family dies, go out and tell the nearest oak tree. That protects *you*!

IF YOU PLANT an oak in the waning of the moon, you will soon receive money. That's definitely better than acorns. Some farmers believe that if oak trees bend in the wind in January, a good crop will be harvested that following autumn. Whether in currency or crops, oak trees bring riches.

WANT TO PROTECT yourself from bewitchment the next time you go hunting? Cut off an oak branch and jump over it with your dogs. Then evil spirits cannot harm you. This only applies to hunters of animals—not those hunting members of the opposite sex for romantic liaisons.

IF YOU HANG a tiny satchel of acorns around a child's neck you will protect the child from harm. Expect your six-year-old to balk at this. Your toddler probably won't put up a fight. If acorn satchels

catch on in the toddler set, this might prove more popular than OshKosh jeans!

———◆———

OAKS AND GODS and goddesses have been lumped together for eons. Most early mythology includes some reference to oak trees: Zeus and Hera; the Scandinavian god, Balder; the Romans' Jupiter; and of course the Druids, were all associated with oak trees. According to some, the name Druid actually means "oak men." In the Judaic-Christian tradition, the Bible records all sorts of events happening under oak trees. From Africa around the world to New Zealand, chances are, whatever your tribe, race, religion, or creed, your ancestors held the oak in high esteem.

———◆———

EVEN IN TWENTIETH century America we have our stories about the oak. It is said that when Franklin Roosevelt's mother died on a windless day in 1941, one of the sturdiest oaks on her Hyde Park estate fell to the ground. You get the picture—the oak tree has been a symbol of reverence and great importance to humans since our brains developed and we started thinking symbolically. Don't mess with oak trees!

◆ Ash to Ash

Ladies, want to know when the right man comes along in your life? Wear an ash leaf in your left hand glove. The first man you meet will become your husband. If you wear an ash leaf in your right glove, the first man you meet will be your lover. And if you wear an ash leaf on your breast, the first man you meet will be the man you love best. I have a difficult time with this superstition. Like many women, I've worked hard to have a variety of choices in my life. I'd rather not let ash leaves make my choices for me!

◆

IN GENERAL, WHETHER you're a man or woman, if you carry an ash leaf in your pocket, purse, knapsack, or even your briefcase, you are protected from evil spirits. Get out there and pick those ash leaves!

◆

SOME COUNTRY FOLKS still believe that wherever an ash grows there are no snakes. Even if you don't have an ash tree growing near your barn and your cow is bitten by a poisonous snake, the ash tree can cure the cow. Make a small wreath of ash twigs and tie it around the neck of the bitten cow. Magically, the ash twigs draw out the snake poison.

◆

LIKEWISE, IF YOU have a sick cow and you think the cow has been bewitched, suspend a branch of the ash tree over the cow's stall. The cow will recuperate. Want to protect your cows from any kind of harm? Tie ash branches to their horns and tails.

◆

IF THE ASH tree doesn't ward off snakes (superstitions don't *always* work) the ash is effective in killing snakes. An old European belief is that one blow from an ash stick will kill an adder—adders are a group of non-poisonous snakes. If you strike an adder with a branch from any other tree, the adder will live until sunset. So always carry an ash stick. No telling when you might come upon a snake in the grass.

—◆—

LOTS OF LEGENDS about ash trees exist. Adam was created out of ash, although the book of Genesis clearly states Adam was made from dust; Zeus created an army of men from ash trees; and according to Norse mythology, humans were first formed from the ash tree. Christian legend says that the baby Jesus was first washed and dressed by the fire of ashwood. However none of the books in the New Testament report this.

—◆—

BESIDES BEING A foe of snakes, ashwood is supposedly good to use in building boats. Mixed with other timber, a boat constructed with some ash never capsizes, according to an old superstition. If you have murky waters to cross in life, it might be wise to have a boat made of ashwood!

◆ Pine Away No More

Did you ever go walking in a pine grove on a windy day and listen to the pines? In Maine we call that sound "whispering pines." Folks in the South call the sound "moans." Some Southerners believe those moans are really the imprisoned spirits of the wind.

◆

THE JAPANESE BELIEVE that, whether whispering or moaning, if a branch of a pine tree grows over your house, you will have continued joy. The pine is a symbol of unflinching purpose and vigorous old age in Japan. Some Japanese once believed the needle-like leaves had the power of driving away demons. Demons, for your information, are global. In all cultures, some people have or had beliefs about demons. It remains to be seen if folks who live on other planets also have beliefs about demons. Demons might just be universal.

◆

IF YOU'RE STANDING under intertwined pine tree branches in any country on our planet and it starts to rain, be careful. If raindrops fall on your head from that nest of pine branches, beware. You will have nightmares that night. So be wary of those raindrops falling on your head.

◆

IN GERMANY IT was once believed you could cure your gout by tieing a knot in the highest shoot of a pine tree. The trick is climbing to the top of the tallest pine tree while you're suffering from the gout! If you can do that, you deserve to live gout-free.

IN ANCIENT PRAGUE, it was believed that if you ate the pine kernel from a cone taken from the topmost branch of the tree, you would be invulnerable to gun shot. If you've climbed the highest pine tree and secured the highest pine cone, you've already proven you're invulnerable to gravity, becoming invulnerable to gun shot is just the next step.

NORSE SHIPS SUPPOSEDLY landed on the coast of Maine long before Columbus landed at the Dominican Republic. Maine offered tall pine trees that made good masts— something the early sailors often needed. Perhaps that's where the belief began that if you cut a pine tree by moonlight it will be water repellent. For your safety, if you go out chopping pines at night (I can think of better things to do at night), make sure it is a clear, moonlit night. One slip of the axe . . .

◆ Willows, Weeping & Otherwise

Want the gift of prophecy? Take 99 leaves from 99 different willow trees. Burn the leaves to ashes. Make the ashes into a powder; eat the powder. Voila, you will have the gift of prophecy. Use it wisely!

◆

MEN, WOMEN—WANT to know if you will soon marry? Throw your shoe at a willow tree on New Year's Day. If your shoe catches on a branch—you will soon marry. If your shoe doesn't catch in your first toss, you can only try a total of nine times. If your shoe doesn't catch after nine times, you're not going to get married within the year. Best to try again next year! A word of advice: Don't use an old shoe. This is too important a matter to leave to an old shoe!

◆

WANT TO CURE that toothache? Stick needles into a willow tree and you will never have another toothache. That's definitely less painful than visiting a dentist! In Japan it's believed by some that the willow is inhabited by a spirit who will cure toothaches. A link might exist here to the modern world. After all, some dentists do behave as though they lived in trees!

◆

IN CHINA WILLOW branches are considered effective charms against evil spirits and diseases caused by evil spirits. There might be some truth to this—aspirin, which seems to cure so many ailments, contains willow bark.

IN IRELAND IT'S believed each willow tree has a soul that speaks in music. This goes along with the general belief that the willow has a soul that dies when you cut it down. It's a belief in many countries that it's unlucky to cut down or burn a willow tree. There is one exception to this belief: If the branches of your willow tree grow up instead of down, cut the tree down. It's an unlucky tree to have in your yard.

—◆—

YOU ARE NOW duly warned: Under no circumstances are your willow branches supposed to grow toward the sky. Why? The legend is that when Adam and Eve were banished from Eden, two angels sat on a willow tree and cried over the couple's misfortune. The angels cried so much their tears ran down the willow's branches and weighed the branches downward, giving the tree the name weeping willow. But weep no more folks—just remember, what's up is up and what's down is down and willow branches grow down!

Part Seven

◆

Four-Footed
Good Luck

If you meet someone who loves animals—they would make a good husband or wife. That really is sound advice! Ladies, if your next date dislikes animals, think twice about him. Likewise men—if your lover doesn't like animals, think twice about marrying her.

He or she who is liked by animals will always have good luck. This makes sense—animals really are good friends to humans.

The Chinese have a belief that if you kill any animal out of sheer cruelty, the animal's soul will take possession of your soul until the crime is completely revenged.

Another superstition, probably told to young children, was that if you touched young puppies and kittens before they gained their sight, your fingernails would turn black. I was taught if I touched newborn puppies, kittens, rabbits, and even chickens, they would be killed by their mother. Something about the scent of human hands would confuse the mother. Needless to say, I never picked up a newborn puppy, kitten, rabbit, or chicken!

Don't let a small animal or bird die in your hand. Bad luck will befall you. In general, it's bad luck to humans when animals die. Primitive folks relied on animals much more than we do today. Human welfare and animal welfare were interwoven.

Today, humans are rather removed from animals. When I lived in a city, I was astonished to meet people who, as children, had never seen cows and pigs. Well, different strokes for different folks, but wherever you live, be kind to animals.

◆ Slow & Steady—Turtles and Tortoises

I t was not a turtle that won the race against the hare. It was a tortoise. Turtles swim in water and walk on the ground. Tortoises are strictly land creatures. But both turtles and tortoises have inspired many superstitions.

◆

CARRY TURTLE BONES in your pocket and you will always have good luck—turtles ward off all sorts of evil. If you do carry turtle bones in your pockets, I suggest you not tell anyone. This is such a little known superstition, they might think you weird!

◆

RUB TURTLE OIL on yourself when you have a fever. There's a catch to this. The oil must come from a turtle that was killed during a waning moon! Though many country folk still keep a jar of turtle oil in the house, it does not have any proven healing value.

◆

IT'S BAD LUCK to own a turtle or tortoise and give it away. But if you carve your initials on its shell, it will never leave you. But don't ever kill a turtle or tortoise unless you intend to eat it. Bad luck comes to those who kill a turtle out of spite.

◆

SOME FOLKS BELIEVE that if a turtle bites you, it will not let go of that bite until it thunders. This could be several days.

◆

TURTLES ALSO PREDICT the weather. If a turtle is on land and its shell is moist, it will soon rain. During a fog take a turtle out of water and put it on the ground right side up. The fog will blow away.

THE TURTLE AND tortoise have long been associated with health and longevity—perhaps because they live a long time. Primitive women wore turtle and tortoise amulets during pregnancy. They believed such amulets were protection from evil and pain in childbirth.

THE CHINESE BELIEVED the tortoise lived 10,000 years and was conceived by thought alone. The Chinese also believed the turtle came out of the Yellow River and a Chinese sage discovered the system of numerals and the basic system of mathematics and philosophy from the turtle's back. The turtle knows what it's about!

TURTLE OR TORTOISE, learn from these creatures. Know what your philosophy in life is and remember—slow and steady is the best course for winning the race—even the rat race!

◆ The Newts in Life

Fortunately, the newt is not a numerous creature, for which I am eternally grateful. Granted, some days the Newt is everywhere, receiving much attention. But the world is not full of Newts. Imagine a world full of Newts . . .

◆

IN IRELAND FOLKS believe that the Irish species of Newt—alpluachra, a species only known in Ireland—jumps down people's throats when it catches folks asleep.

◆

OF COURSE IN the U.S. we have the Georgia Newt, once thought ridiculous and harmless. Now we realize Newts are quite powerful and have a tight network. It's said that the Georgia Newt jumps down anyone's throat, whether asleep or not, with a special penchant for attacking single mothers.

◆

IN MALTA FOLKS believe if a child kills a Newt and its tail keeps wagging, that tail will be the curse of the child's parents. What happens if the child has only one parent is lost knowledge, but we might soon rediscover that knowledge.

NEWTS ARE SMALL, slender creatures with four weak legs and a flat tail. The creature is really an amphibian. Newts hatch under water. As the little Newts grow, they develop powerful lungs, capable of holding vast amounts of hot air. (Georgian Newts excel in this department.) After their lungs develop is when they take the land—or rather take to the land. Most people call them efts when they are walking on land. (Other people call them Republicans.)

—◆—

NEWTS/EFTS SHED THEIR skin many times, and it is reported that if they lose a leg, they can grow it back. Newts do have incredible comebacks.

—◆—

OTHER ANIMALS STAY away from the water-type Newt and the land-type efts. Their skin is poisonous and they are known to have mean tongues. Beware of Newts!

◆ Frogs and Toads A Hopping

It is good luck if a frog or toad enters your house—a four-legged frog or toad. The frog was sacred to Ptah—a most ancient of gods. Ptah was the creator of everything. It's still bad luck to kill a frog. Some farm folks still believe that if you kill a frog it makes cow's milk bloody. Relax, there is no truth to this!

———◆———

FROGS CAN CURE the gout. Find a frog on a gray, overcast day or cloudy night. No sunshine or moonlight must shine on Earth for this charm to work. Cut off the frog's hind legs. Wrap each leg in deerskin. Apply the right leg of the frog to your right foot. Apply the left leg of the frog to your left foot. Your gout will be healed.

———◆———

IF ON YOUR way to a dice game you meet a frog on the road, you will win money in the game. If you wish on the first frog you see in spring, and keep the wish a secret, it will come true. If you hear frogs croaking, it will soon rain.

———◆———

FROGS ARE THE symbol of fertility—perhaps because of the enormous number of eggs they lay. In Rome folks wore frog charms that supposedly gave them the power to keep love and attract friends.

———◆———

NOTE: FROGS AND toads are different. The frog has teeth and breathes through its skin. Its legs are longer than a toad's and it lays eggs in a clump. The toad doesn't breath through its skin. It has short legs and lays its eggs in a string.

$$\blacklozenge$$

IF YOU FIND a toad in the cellar, it brings bad luck. Be careful how you get rid of it. Gypsies believe a tame toad brings good luck. Unfortunately, I do not have any tips on how to tame a toad. If you see many toads in August, it is a sign of a plentiful harvest.

$$\blacklozenge$$

IN FAIRY TALES, a frog, not a toad, often turns into a prince when kissed by a woman. I doubt that will happen today. A prince is a rare commodity. But if you're a single lady and you kiss a frog, it might just turn into a New Age sensitive man!

◆ Slippery, Slimy Snakes

Snakes are not slippery or slimy, nor are they evil. Seeing a snake does not portend bad luck. Snakes can bring good luck and bad. Your bad luck can often be brought on by your bad attitude toward reptiles.

———◆———

A SNAKE CANNOT put its tail in its mouth to form a hoop, roll after you, knock you down, and kill you. Neither can a snake hypnotize you and then give you a poisonous bite. Nor does a snake sting with its tongue. All of the above are unfounded medieval superstitions.

———◆———

THE EARLY EGYPTIANS worshipped snakes and thought them immortal—perhaps because they watched snakes molt. A drawing of a snake with its tail in its mouth was the symbol of eternity. And the symbol for healing, the caduceus, has two snakes entertwined, indicating harmony—long believed a necessary ingredient for healing in life. Unfortunately, these days few doctors stress harmony as a key to good health—even though the medical symbol is still the caduceus.

———◆———

THAT SNAKES ONLY die after sunset is a common belief today. At least folks now realize snakes die! Another prevalent superstition is that if a tree dies, it has been struck by a snake's tail's sting. There is absolutely no truth in this. A snake cannot kill a tree! Nor do snakes travel in pairs. They are loners by nature. Just like some people I know!

———◆———

RATTLESNAKES ARE A type of poisonous snake in North America. The belief that a rattler with no fangs is harmless is erroneous. Rattlers shed their fangs twice a year, but even without visible fangs, rattlers are dangerous.

◆

WHEN CAMPING, COWBOYS once only slept within a circle of their lariat. They believed that rattlers would not crawl over a hair rope—most ropes were once made of horse hair or cow hair. Sleeping within a circle of branches or rope is an old custom—supposedly the circle protects against danger. But be warned—if you're camping and sleeping on the ground in rattlesnake country, a rope circle will not protect you. Best to sleep in a tent!

◆ More Than Milk—Cows

W hen I was a kid, every summer weekend we drove from the small Massachusetts town where we lived to a camp on a mountain in mid-Vermont. In those days Vermont had more cows than people, so we saw lots of cows. If the cows were lying down, inevitably, my mother would announce it was going to rain. She learned that superstition from her mother. Now I pass it on to the kids I know.

———◆———

BUT FOR EVERY one person I've met who believes it will rain when cows are lying down in the pasture, I've met an equal number of people who say that if cows are lying down in the pasture on a wet day, it is a sign the weather will clear! And everyone agrees it's good luck if cows lie down on Christmas Day.

Where, how, and why folks got it into their heads that if cows lie down in the pasture, it will rain, I've never been able to unearth. Of course, fifty percent of the time these folks are right and it does rain. Fifty percent of the time they're wrong. But I often think folks are more successful predicting the weather based on what the cows are doing than TV weather forecasters who use satellite photos and jet streams.

———◆———

COWS ARE SACRED creatures in Egypt and India, and it's no wonder. They are magnificent, gentle creatures, and when you consider how much milk they produce, generous. Cows were not indigenous to North America. They arrived here in the fifteenth century with the Spanish explorers.

171

COWS GET ATTACHED to their owners. We've all heard stories about a cow that was sold to the farmer down the road, but every evening returned to her original owner. It's no wonder then there are beliefs about cows and their owners. If a cow lies down on Christmas Day, for example, it does not mean rain. It means good luck for the owner of the cow.

BUT IT'S BAD luck for the owner if one cow licks the forehead of another. That portends the death of the owner. And if a cow does not bawl when its calf is sold, there will be a death in the family that owns the cow.

IF A FARMER'S best cow dies, it means the strongest member of the family will soon die. And if a cow's shadow comes between you and the sky, that's an omen of your death! Likewise, if a cow licks one of the windows of a house, it's an omen someone in the house will die. Frankly, I think it's a sign something is wrong with the cow!

BY THE WAY, a cure for the cow that always runs home to its original owner is to cut off a piece of the cow's tail. The cow will never run away again—it's some sort of belief about the tail wagging the cow!

◆ Goats—Scapegoats & All

Goats, unfortunately, get bad press. In the Bible and in children's stories such as "The Three Billy Goats Gruff," goats are cast as ornery, stubborn garbage eaters. Goats are none of these. Goats are wonderful, curious creatures who eat only brushwood and weeds. In fact, they have a great ability to clear brush land. They are nature's lawn mowers!

◆

A GOAT ON a farm brings good luck to the farmer. Traditionally goats are kept in horse stables in the belief that goats preserve horses from diseases. How this is done no one can explain. It just happens!

◆

IF YOU MEET a four-legged goat just before starting a new business venture, you will have success. I don't know how this superstition holds up during a recession, however.

◆

IF YOU MIX the bile of a black goat with your saliva, you have a mixture that is supposed to cure everything from headaches to in-grown toenails! It's best to pass this one by, though.

◆

PUT A GOAT'S horns under your pillow if you have insomnia. But be sure to lay the horns sideways. Otherwise you might get a punctured ear drum.

◆

THE SCAPEGOAT OR "escape" goat has an ancient history—all part of the bad press. Traditionally the scapegoat carries the burden of human sin. The Greeks, Romans, and Hebrews practiced this belief.

173

In Leviticus the fate of two goats is recorded. One goat was sacrificed as a sin offering. The other goat was presented live to God for atonement and then led into the wilderness. This became the ritual for ancient Israelites on their Day of Atonement. The goat is, however, an innocent creature. Why it is the dumping ground for human sin is a mystery.

◆

BUT PICASSO DID much to raise the status of goats. He created a wonderful sculpture of a pregnant goat and called it *The People*!

◆ Pigs—Tails & Squeals

Overall, pigs bring good luck—and you thought they were only good for ham and bacon. Today most folks tend to think of pigs in negative ways—as scuffy and dirty. But primitive folks believed pigs had supernatural powers.

◆

PIGS ARE TABOO to the Hindus and the Hebrews. If a Hindu eats a pig after it has been offered for sacrifice, the Hindu must die.

◆

FOR MANY OTHER cultures, however, the pig means good luck. A widely held superstition is that if you meet a herd of hogs in your day's travels, you will have good luck. And if a bridal couple about to begin their honeymoon encounters a herd of pigs, the couple will have great good luck.

◆

TO BREAK A spell of bad luck, pull a pig's tail. That is, if you can catch a pig. They tend to run from people. To make a pig fatter, cut off its tail—so say the oldtimers.

◆

IF THE FIRST time you drive pigs outside you make them jump over your apron, the pigs will always come home. Getting a pig to jump over anything is a feat. Besides, who wears an apron these days? Beware—if you first drive pigs to pasture on a Wednesday, they will never come home. You can, however, paste a leaf from the Bible over their sty before you take them to pasture, then the pigs will not roam. I suggest you don't paste Matthew 7:6; the pigs might trample you, pearls or no pearls.

IF YOU BUY a pig on credit it will grunt until it's paid for. But there's little chance of buying a pig on credit. Pig dealers rarely take MasterCard, AmericanExpress, or even Visa Gold.

IF PIGS GIVE funny whines, watch out for a calamity. And if pigs squeal loudly, it means a storm is approaching. Supposedly pigs can *see* the wind. Remember, though, pigs tend to squeal when they are hungry (which is often), so if you don't feed them on time, they might start predicting a storm.

A SIMILAR BELIEF is that if pigs squeal a lot, there will be a high wind. This belief that pigs can see the wind is universal. Read Byron's epic poem *Don Juan*—"Ask the pig who sees the wind."

A FAMILY IS bound to come down with the flu (despite flu shots), if all of its pigs run away. It's more likely such a luckless family will have a lean winter.

TO HAVE THE best ham and bacon, slaughter a pig on the rising of the moon. If you kill a pig when the moon is waning you'll have rancid bacon—you won't want to bring home that bacon!

◆ Sheep—Shearing & Counting

Mary's little lamb who followed her to school one day was really not that unusual. Lambs make good pets. I know a couple who kept a lamb as a pet and it lived in their house!

◆

SHEEP HAVE COME to symbolize self-sacrifice, perhaps because primitive people were always sacrificing sheep to their gods. But take note: Sheep are not subservient and can be quite feisty. Sheep can also mean good luck.

◆

DID YOU KNOW that it's good luck to meet a flock of sheep on your way to work? It's bad luck to pass through a flock of sheep. Better to relinquish the right of way. Of course, not many of us are likely to run into a flock of sheep on our way to work these days!

◆

IF A BRIDAL party meets a flock of sheep on the way to the church, that means good luck and prosperity for the couple.

◆

IF SHEEP STAND with their back to the wind, expect a cold spell. This superstition isn't specific about snow or sleet—just a cold spell. Best to get out your sheepskin!

◆

SHEAR SHEEP DURING the rising moon. You will produce stronger wool. The connection between the moon and fleece is lost knowledge. But if you have a corn on your toe, take a piece of that wool just sheared and place it on your corn. Within a week the corn will fall off. Wool was the forerunner of Dr. Scholls' medicated corn pads!

IF A EWE has two black lambs, bad luck is in the air. This was such a pervasive superstition, many farmers used to cut the throats of black lambs before they could bleat their first baa. Fortunately that's not the custom today.

IF YOU CAN'T get to sleep, it's recommended to count sheep with your eyes closed. But if you dream of sheep once you get to sleep, watch out. You will have bad luck. Just to be on the safe side, instead of counting sheep, have a cup of herbal tea before going to bed. Herbal tea is as old a remedy for insomnia as counting sheep.

◆ Neighing Horses

Horses were once as important to people as cars are today. We tell stories at potluck suppers about car dealers; our forebears told stories about horse traders. And superstitions about horses run the gamut from a horse's color to horses' rubbing their heads together.

◆

UNFORTUNATELY, MAJOR TECHNOLOGICAL advances such as the internal combustion engine, computers, copying machines, the fax machine, and TVs (the whole technological highway), seem to have only inspired a general superstition about creatures everyone calls gremlins.

Gremlins are microscopic (not macroscopic) creatures that live in the above-named machines. Usually when use of the machines is intense—near the closing of a deadline, a "big deal," or a live TV show—they malfunction. Gremlins cause such malfunctions. Gremlins decide at random when to "gum up the works." To reverse the gremlin effect, press buttons on the machine and/or bang on the machine's case. This scares off the gremlins. When gremlins invade a car's engine, the counter-effect is to get out and kick the tires.

◆

BUT BACK TO horses. Make a wish when you see a spotted horse. Also, if you see a chestnut horse with two white feet and a white nose, you soon will have very good luck.

◆

SUPERSTITIONS ABOUT WHITE horses vary. Some say it's unlucky to meet a white horse. To avoid the bad luck, spit at the horse. In Massachusetts, when you see a white horse, spit over the little finger on your right hand and you will always have money! But if you see a man creep under the head of a white horse—beware—he's a shady businessman. But do stop and think; have you ever seen your banker creep under the head of a white horse? Point of information: No reference is made to businesswomen's being shady.

———◆———

TO KEEP YOUR horse healthy and free from disease, clip its mane at night during a full moon. Best not to do this on a cloudy night, but when the moonlight is clear. You do want to see what you're doing.

———◆———

IT'S BAD LUCK to witness two horses rubbing their heads together. Why? Who knows—just look the other way. It's a private moment and horses, too, need privacy.

———◆———

NEIGHING HORSES GET a mixed review. To hear one horse neigh is a sign of good luck. And if a horse neighs when an unmarried woman passes by, that woman will be married within the year.

———◆———

PAY ATTENTION TO this one: To hear a horse neigh after it has drunk water is bad luck. You *can* lead a horse to water, but you *can't* make it drink. However, if sooner or later it gets thirsty (which is likely), you *can* watch it drink—but after it drinks, you *can't* listen to it neigh!

———◆———

IF A HORSE shies in front of a house, there is trouble in that house. There's probably truth in that; animals can sense trouble.

———◆———

AND THIS GRIM one—if horses run and play in the pasture, it's an omen someone in the house will die—is absurd. Horses, especially colts, were born to be frisky. Some folks believe that if you see a colt coming toward you it's a sign of good luck—that's a four-legged colt, not the Plymouth/Dodge Colt.

—◆—

ONE GENEROUS SUPERSTITION is that if you give a horse to a friend, you insure everlasting friendship. But this depends on where the friend lives. If she or he lives in a high-rise in Chicago, your friend might not appreciate receiving a horse—and there goes the friendship. Better to give your friend a fax machine—that way you can easily communicate.

◆ Clucking Hens & Crowing Roosters

Hens and roosters. Where would the world be without them? Hungry, no doubt. No one knows when hens and roosters were first domesticated. They and superstitions about them seem to have been with us since the beginning of time.

◆

HENS WERE USED by Roman oracles for divination. The gizzards were studied to predict the future about love, battles (and love-battles), politics, and babies. But we won't get into cutting up chickens here. We'll stick to the less messy superstitions.

◆

GENERALLY IF A hen roosts at noonday that's a sign someone in the family will soon die. And anyone who has the blood of a chicken spilled on their clothes will die an unnatural death. So when you're killing your chickens be careful.

◆

THE CLUCKING OF a hen near a patient's bed is a sign of death. But what are hens doing in the house anyway? It's not advisable to let hens in your house—despite the belief that it's good luck for a hen and her chicks to stray into your house.

◆

WATCH OUT FOR mean gossip about you if you see two hens fighting. Gossips can be as mean as hens, and gossip seems a worldwide pastime. People obviously don't have enough to do—idle hands make for mean mouths. But take note—if people are talking *about* you, chances are those people are not talking *to* you. Gossips never talk to the person they're gossiping about. And would you *want* to talk to those people?

IF YOU SEE hens laying eggs, you will have good luck—maybe those gossips will be struck dumb!

IF YOU TIE an old tough hen to a fig tree, the hen will become tender. I wouldn't count on this superstition when you're planning Sunday dinner for your in-laws. Best to go buy a fresh, young chicken.

OF COURSE THERE are a number of superstitions about hens clucking and roosters crowing. Let's not forget the rooster—where would the hen be without the rooster and the rooster without the hen? The same is true of men and women. Maybe we humans should take note of that and call a truce to gender fighting.

IN KOREA IT'S unlucky if you hear a rooster crow at sunset and a hen cluck at night. In Africa it's unlucky for a rooster to crow before midnight. Roosters and hens do all their talking in daytime and it's just unnatural for these creatures to be making  noises at night. They are "light sensitive" creatures. During a solar eclipse hens will go to roost, and when the light comes back roosters will crow. Think what ancients must have thought of solar eclipses! We do know ancients thought it unlucky to eat a rooster. It's also tough going!

IF A ROOSTER crows when your guest is leaving—even if it's daybreak—that guest will soon die, so say folks in Germany. But if a rooster crows in your cellar door—even at daybreak—it's a sign of a speedy marriage. So when your guests are leaving at daybreak make sure all your roosters are standing in your cellar door.

◆

IF A ROOSTER crows all day, expect rain. If a rooster comes into your house it's a sign strangers will visit—probably the Board of Health!

◆

AND THE END of all ends of a superstition: when all the roosters in the world stop crowing, the end of the world is at hand. Beware! Repent!

◆ Fox Lungs & Fur

D o you want to increase your chances of winning that marathon? Eat fox lungs! It sounds awful—but primitive people believed eating fox lungs strengthened breathing. After all, they saw that foxes were excellent runners, and rarely were out of breath!

◆

IF A FOX has thick fur in the autumn, it will be a severe winter. This is an overall superstition for all fur animals. But when you hear a fox bark in March, know that winter is over and spring is near. That's a rather safe prediction!

◆

IF YOU HEAR a fox bark in other months of the year, someone close to you will die. A fox can see death approaching. It is eerie to hear a fox bark in the night, and it sets off expectations of all sorts of evil doings.

◆

NO SUCH CREATURE exists as the flying fox. What folks call a flying fox is really a species of bat.

◆

IN JAPAN FOXES are lucky animals, but in most countries foxes mean bad luck. If you see a fox, lots of people believe you will meet swindlers shortly. And it's a bad sign to see a fox howling and crying along the road. If you have to fight a fox, you will soon have to fight a cunning enemy. It's also a bad omen to see a white fox.

◆

GENERALLY WHEN A fox shrieks and barks it means danger. In Maine the story goes that a man was chopping a tree; he stopped to rest and heard a fox shriek. Before he could chop anymore, the tree fell and killed him.

—◆—

MANY WOMEN BELIEVE that to be called a vixen is an insult. Not necessarily true. A vixen is faithful and stands by her mate through good times and bad. She fights for her young when they are in danger. To be called a vixen is really a compliment!

◆ The Four-Footed Wolf

Feared and revered; that's the story of the wolf. In Russia the wolf is honored. In most countries, the wolf is disparaged, and in the U.S. it has almost become extinct.

Wolves can be scary creatures because of the way they howl—and they always seem to howl in the Hollywood movies when people are at the most desolate time in their lives. Wolves seem to represent bad luck and vulnerability.

———◆———

MANY FOLKS BELIEVE that if you suffer from insomnia, put a wolf's head under your pillow and you'll sleep peacefully and safely. Make sure it's a *cleaned* wolf's head.

———◆———

THE ANCIENTS BELIEVED if you put wolf's milk on your skin it would purify it, acting as a deep cleansing elixir. But it's hard to come by; would you catch a wolf and milk it?

———◆———

THAT'S THE REVERENCE given to wolves. There are also superstitions born out of fear. In Portugal, if you're out and about and see a wolf (the four-legged kind, not the human kind), bad luck is in your future. If you're out in the woods and a wolf sees you before you see the wolf, you'll be struck dumb. Beware of wolves!

———◆———

LOTS OF SUPERSTITIONS exist about how to counter a wolf's evil. Sprinkle salt on the tracks of a wolf and the wolf will run away. If you see a wolf carrying off your lamb or pig, let something fall from your dress or pants pocket, and the wolf will drop its prey.

OF COURSE ALL these superstitions are about the canine species of wolves. We women have superstitions about two-legged wolves. Don't have anything to do with a two-legged creature who has big ears, sharp teeth, and a very hairy body. And if you ever comment to a guy that he has big eyes and he replies, "All the better to see you with, my dear . . ."—watch out; remember, a wolf is a wolf is a wolf.

◆ Dogs—Friends Indeed

When American soldiers were off fighting Desert Storm, my friend George watched the war on television. Molly, his Scottish terrier, sat at his feet. After a few moments of the television war, Molly would sit up, howl, and pace around the den barking. One evening George decided not to watch the war. Molly did not howl or bark all evening. George never watched the war again. George is convinced Molly howled and barked because she sensed death.

◆

THE GREEKS BELIEVED dogs howled and barked when the goddess Hecate was present. Hecate was the goddess of witchcraft, darkness, and terror, and could only be seen by dogs. Dogs always tried to warn humans of her presence.

◆

IT IS UNLUCKY for a dog to howl in your yard—that means the dog sees your coffin. If a dog howls with its nose to the ground it's an omen of death. If a dog howls under the window of a sick person, that person will die soon. Dogs also give warning of death by scratching at your door.

◆

WHETHER DOGS SEE death or not, dogs do hear danger long before humans do. A dog's hearing range is sixteen times that of a human.

◆

IT'S CONSIDERED BAD luck in many countries—Japan, China, Egypt, Persia—to kill a dog. And if you kick a dog, your knees will grow too large for your legs!

GOOD LUCK IS yours if you are followed by a stray dog. But bad luck is yours if the stray dog follows you on a rainy night. Beware of the visitor to your house if your dog refuses to make friends with the man or woman. That's sound advice; animals can sense mean people.

THE OLD BELIEF that dogs are man's (and woman's) best friend has some truth. Dogs have been known to sit for months on the gravesites of their dead masters and mistresses. And remember Argos—Ulysses' dog. Argos waited twenty years for his master to return. Ulysses returned in disguise, but Argos, even though aged, recognized Ulysses, jumped up and wagged his tail, as dogs do when they are happy.

THE OLD BELIEF that a dog will bite the hand that feeds it is a falsehood. The majority of dogs make good pets, and have since wild dogs were first tamed over sixty thousand years ago. Today dogs are even used to sniff out illegal drugs—that's certainly proof dogs are humans' best friends!

◆ Squirrelly Squirrels

S quirrels, in the world of superstition, are known as exemplary
weather forecasters. Some folks even claim they are better at
predicting the weather than the *Old Farmers' Almanac*!
Here are some hints for what the forecast will be.

◆

IF IN AUTUMN you have only a few squirrels in your backyard
raiding your bird feeders, it will be a hard winter. Of course, the
squirrels might have moved on to another backyard because they don't
like the food you put out for the birds. Squirrels can be picky eaters.

◆

IF IN THE autumn you notice squirrels putting in a large food
supply, it's going to be a long and cold winter. But be advised,
squirrels always put up lots of provisions. That's where the
expression "squirreling" came from!

◆

SQUIRRELS SOMEHOW ALSO became the great protector
against fire. In medieval times, squirrels were kept as caged pets in
houses. This protected the houses from fire. How squirrels became
associated with fire is anyone's guess. They do, however, dart and
leap, much like the flames of a bonfire.

◆

IN RURAL EUROPE at the traditional Easter bonfire, squirrels were
burned. Shepherds even forced their sheep to jump over the squirrel
fire. This was supposed to protect the sheep from evil and disease.

◆

PEOPLE DON'T BURN squirrels today—instead they feed them. I
am one of those people! The squirrels in my yard like peanuts
(shelled or unshelled), walnuts, and chunky peanut butter!

191

◆ The Cat's Meow

No book on superstitions would be complete without a mention of the cat. Whether worshipped or scorned, throughout history cats have always inspired superstitions and legends. In ancient Egypt cats were worshipped and, according to legend, cats eliminated a plague of rats in Egypt. Egyptians not only mummified their dead pharaohs, but also their dead cats.

◆

IN THE DARK Ages cats were mistrusted and believed to consort with witches and warlocks. They brought evil and bad luck. Some folks reason that the bubonic plague that killed thousands of people in Europe during the medieval ages was caused by killing the then believed "evil cats." In killing the cats, people killed the natural predator of rats—the creatures who spread the plague.

◆

TODAY SUPERSTITIONS ABOUT cats are still handed down from generation to generation. Many folks still believe if a black cat crosses your path, you are in for bad luck.

◆

IF A CAT washes its ears, bad weather is on the way. Or if a cat licks its tail, it will rain. Of course there is no truth to these beliefs. Cats always wash their ears and tail. Cats are by nature clean animals. They are, as I've often pointed out to my friends, always doing their own laundry.

◆

IF THE FIRST person a cat looks at after washing itself is young and single that person will marry soon. Remember, for this superstition to work, you have to be young and single. This does not apply to middle-aged folks!

◆

IT'S GOOD LUCK for a couple getting married that a cat be present at their wedding. My friend Jenny happened to live next door to the church where she was married. She didn't invite her cat Sam to her wedding. In fact she didn't pay much attention to Sam at all on the day of her wedding. But Sam went to the wedding anyway; he sat by the door during the ceremony. Later, at the reception in the church undercroft, Sam sat by Jenny when the haddock luncheon was served! The couple is happily married to this day!

◆

IF YOU THROW a cat overboard while on a boat, a storm will blow up. If you throw a cat into the sea, you deserve to have a storm blow up. Why would anyone be so mean?

◆

GENERALLY, IT'S BAD luck to kill a cat—even today after all those anti-cat beliefs during medieval times. And if you're mean to a cat and kick it, the cat will get its revenge by stealing your chickens. So watch out. Protect your chickens.

◆

BLACK CATS SPAWNED a variety of superstitions. If a black cat comes to your door, you will soon have a lover in your life. If a black cat adopts you, you will have bad luck, so send it away. If a black cat lies on a grave it means the dead person's soul is possessed by the devil. And if you stroke a black cat's tail seven times you will have good luck in cards.

◆

WHEREAS HAVING A white cat means poverty, having a black cat means wealth. And if you see a white cat on a full moon, it means you will soon be married.

IF YOU CUT a cat's whiskers, the cat will be blind. There is no truth to this. A cat's whiskers are feelers. Whiskers tell a cat how tight a spot it's in!

A CAT SUCKS a baby's breath away. This superstition is from the Dark Ages. A cat cannot and does not "take" a baby's breath away. In fact, cats like babies and will often sleep at the bottom of their cribs the way they will sleep at the end of their master's or mistress's bed.

REMEMBER, CATS ARE wonderfully independent creatures; they obey no one. Because they are not obedient, in some circles they have a bad reputation—similar to independent women. But what kind of world would it be without cats—or independent women?